AMARG
America's Military Aircraft Boneyard

Nicholas A. Veronico and Ron Strong

specialtypress
PUBLISHERS AND WHOLESALERS

Specialty Press
39966 Grand Avenue
North Branch, MN 55056
Phone: 651-277-1400 or 800-895-4585
Fax: 651-277-1203
www.specialtypress.com

Edit by Mike Machat
Layout by Monica Seiberlich

ISBN 978-1-58007-139-0
Item No. SP139

Library of Congress Cataloging-in-Publication Data

Veronico, Nick
  AMARG : America's military aircraft boneyard / by Nicholas A. Veronico and Ron Strong.
    p. cm.
  Includes bibliographical references and index.
  ISBN 978-1-58007-139-0
  1. Aerospace Maintenance and Regeneration Group (U. S.)—History. 2. Airplanes, Military—United States—Maintenance and repair. 3. Airplanes, Military—United States—History. 4. Davis-Monthan Air Force Base (Ariz.)—History. 5. Pima Air & Space Museum. I. Strong, Ron. II. Title.
  UG1243.V468 2010
  358.4'175—dc22

                2009032811

Printed in China
10 9 8 7 6 5 4 3

For Becky and Betty

Front Cover:

The first Rockwell B-1B to arrive at AMARG touched down on 20 August 2002. In a cost-saving effort, the Air Force's B-1 fleet was reduced from 92 aircraft to 60, with 8 going to various museums and 24 to the storage facility. Ten of the 24 stored B-1Bs will be kept intact, while the remaining aircraft have been subjected to the parts reclamation process to keep other aircraft flying. (Nicholas A. Veronico)

Title Page:

More than 30 engineless Douglas C-124 Globemaster IIs line up for an appointment with the scrapper's blade. Of the more than 200 C-124s that flew into the storage facility, only two were sent back out to museums (49-0236 to Pima Air & Space Museum, Tucson, and 52-1066 to the National Museum of the U.S. Air Force, Wright-Patterson AFB, Ohio). (National Archives)

Back Cover Photos

Left:

The legendary Grumman Tomcat's motto was always "Anytime, baby!" However, time has finally run out for this F-14B that last served with VF-32 Swordsmen onboard the USS Harry S. Truman (CVN-75). Tomcat 162691 is seen here wearing a retro scheme applied especially for the type's phase-out as VF-32 transitioned into the new Boeing F/A-18F Super Hornet. (Ron Strong)

Right:

Aerial view of the Boeing B-52 fleet's geometrically precise parking arrangement. These aircraft are patiently awaiting their final fate, whether it be donating parts to keep the other 50-plus-year-old Stratofortresses in the air or perhaps a solemn date with the scrapper's torch. (Nicholas A. Veronico)

OVERSEAS DISTRIBUTION BY:

PGUK
63 Hatton Garden
London EC1N 8LE, England
Phone: 020 7061 1980 • Fax: 020 7242 3725
www.pguk.co.uk

Renniks Publications Ltd.
3/37-39 Green Street
Banksmeadow, NSW 2109, Australia
Phone: 2 9695 7055 • Fax: 2 9695 7355
www.renniks.com

TABLE OF CONTENTS

Acknowledgments...4

About the Authors..4

Introduction 5

Chapter One: Developing A Strategic Aircraft Reserve...........................6

Chapter Two: Aircraft Storage and Disposal 26

Chapter Three: Along the Storage Rows 52

Chapter Four: Scrapping the Big Fleets 106

Appendix 141
    Inventory by Aircraft Type (2009)..141
    Boneyard Tours and the Pima Air & Space Museum 142

Bibliography and Suggested Reading 143

Acknowledgments

Delving into the histories of so many aircraft over such a tremendous time span has meant drawing upon the talents and knowledge of many organizations, groups, and individuals. We would like to thank the following for their assistance: Kelly and Ian Abbott, Brian Baker, Beth Barksdale and the staff of the Pima Air & Space Museum, Allan Blue, Caroline and Ray Bingham, Steve Birdsall, Claire and Joe Bradshaw, Darlene and Roger Cain, John M. Campbell, Rob Chilcoat, Dan Collier, Ed Davies, Robert F. Dorr, Candy and Wayman Dunlap—*Pacific Flyer*, Jim Dunn, Desirae Fromayan, Jerry Fugere, Scott E. Germain, Wayne McPherson Gomes, Jackie and A. Kevin Grantham, K. B. Haack, Todd Hackbarth, Dan Hagedorn, Ted Holgerson, Earl Holmquist, Dennis Jenkins, Frederick Johnsen, Norm Jukes, Phil Kortas, Nancy and Robert A. Kropp, Tillie and William T. Larkins, Gerald Liang, Mike Machat, Yvonne and Dale Messimer, Ken Miller, Gina Morello, Linda and Dan O'Hara, Milo Peltzer, Taigh Ramey, Harrison Rued, Darrel Scent, Rhonda and Doug Scroggins, Becky, Brett, and Aaron Strong, Linda Terrin—Mohave County Historical Society, Lisa and Scott Thompson, Rick Turner, Terry Vanden-Heuvel—AMARG, Richard H. VanderMuelen, Betty S. Veronico, Karen and Armand H. Veronico, Kathleen and Tony Veronico.

Nicholas A. Veronico
San Carlos, California

Ron Strong
Dublin, California

About the Authors

Nicholas A. Veronico and Ron Strong share a great interest in aviation. The friends both got their start in aviation journalism with *Pacific Flyer* in the mid 1980s, and now work on the same project at NASA Ames Research Center in Mountain View, California.

Nicholas A. Veronico is a science and technology writer who works for the Astronomical Society of the Pacific at the Stratospheric Observatory for Infrared Astronomy (SOFIA) Science Center at NASA Ames. He is the author of more than two-dozen books on military and aviation subjects, and served as the lead scriptwriter for *Scrapping Aircraft Giants*, a Discovery Channel documentary on commercial aircraft scrapping. *AMARG: America's Military Aircraft Boneyard* is his fifth book for Specialty Press.

Ron Strong always had an interest in aircraft. As a child growing up in Burbank, California, his father worked for different airlines and would take the family to airports and air shows in the region. While serving in the Air Force, Strong worked on aircraft with the 53rd Weather Reconnaissance Squadron, Ramey Air Force Base, Puerto Rico, and with a Special Operations Squadron on Combat Talon and Spectre Gunships at Hurlburt Field, Florida. He later worked at the Alameda Naval Air Rework Facility in Flight Test. For the past 25 years, he has worked for NASA performing wind tunnel testing on civilian aircraft. The last eight years at NASA have been spent working on the SOFIA program. Strong has more than 40 years experience in aviation photography.

INTRODUCTION

The sight of thousands of aircraft, parked wingtip to wingtip, in the heat of the desert is something to behold. The interest of many was piqued by glossy black-and-white images of combat veteran World War II fighters and bombers sitting at places like Kingman and Davis-Monthan AFB, Arizona, in the 1940s, and Litchfield Park, also in Arizona, in the 1950s. Traveling to the Sonoran Desert to view the military's aircraft storage center has become somewhat of a sacred pilgrimage for aviation enthusiasts.

What is today's military aircraft storage center started out after the end of World War II storing B-29s and C-47s as a strategic reserve should America need access to additional bombing and troop transport assets. These aircraft were managed by the 4105th Army Air Force Base Unit (Air Base). In 1948, the 4105th's designation was changed to the 3040th Aircraft Storage Depot, later Aircraft Storage Squadron, which played a major role in returning B-29s and C-47s for the fight against communist aggression during the Korean War. As the Cold War heated up, on 1 June 1956, the 3040th was renamed the Arizona Aircraft Storage Branch (AASB), and three years later was redesignated the 2704th Air Force Aircraft Storage and Disposition Group.

In 1964, the government's efforts to reduce operational duplication between the military services saw all aircraft storage consolidated at Davis-Monthan under the 2704th. Navy, Marine Corps, and Coast Guard aircraft in storage at Litchfield Park, outside Phoenix, Arizona, worthy of being retained in the inventory were moved 150 miles south to Davis-Monthan. Those that were obsolete were eliminated. Having consolidated the aircraft storage function, the 2704th was renamed to more accurately reflect its new managerial role, and on 1 February 1965, became known as the Military Aircraft Storage and Disposition Center (MASDC).

To further align the center's name with the services it provided, in October 1985 MASDC became the Aerospace Maintenance and Regeneration Center, or AMARC. After two wars, numerous military conflicts, the end of the Cold War, and an unprecedented military drawdown, on 3 May 2007, AMARC became the 309th Aerospace Maintenance and Regeneration Group (309 AMARG) reporting to the 309th Maintenance Wing at Hill Air Force Base, Utah. The 309th Maintenance Wing manages all aspects of depot-level repair and maintenance for the A-10, C-130, F-16, and F-22, at the Ogden Air Logistics Center, Hill AFB, Utah. This realignment brings AMARG into the Air Force's squadron structure and streamlines many procedures including budget.

Having such a long history and a great number of name changes, we have chosen to use "Davis-Monthan" and "AMARG" interchangeably to represent the aircraft storage and maintenance facility.

Each visit is like entering a time capsule for military aircraft historians, modelers, and hobbyists. Aircraft markings, external configurations, and the operational histories of individual air and rotorcraft are what draw visitors. And with more than 4,000 aircraft in an ever-changing state of storage, every experience is different.

CHAPTER ONE

DEVELOPING A STRATEGIC AIRCRAFT RESERVE

More than 5,400 aircraft were parked at Kingman, Arizona, at the conclusion of hostilities, and many of the aircraft could be seen by motorists cruising along Route 66. Easily identifiable in this extremely rare color photo are two B-17s. Douglas-built B-17G-50-DL 44-6448 served with the 96th Bomb Squadron (Circle Y for the 15th Air Force, 2nd Bomb Group) at Amendola, Italy, wore the names Hubba Hubba *and* Big Nose, *and flew 49 missions before the war ended. B-17G-70-BO 43-37797 served with the 708th Bomb Squadron (Square K for the 8th Air Force, 447th Bomb Group), and was named* American Beauty. *Both aircraft arrived at Kingman on 14 December 1945. (Jerry McLain via Steve Birdsall)*

The conclusion of World War II saw the U.S. Army Air Forces faced with a unique situation. By the end of 1945, more than 30,000 surplus aircraft were choking storage fields around the country, the jet engine was coming of age, and America's enemy was changing from fascists to communists. The jet engine and forthcoming jet-powered fighters and bombers quickly made many of the war's frontline aircraft, like the P-38, P-39, and P-63 fighters, and B-17 and B-24 bombers, obsolete.

By comparison, at the end of World War I, thousands of surplus aircraft and aircraft components, such as engines, were dumped onto the American civil aviation market. This made for cheap aircraft; however, the massive surplus aircraft stocks strangled the market for newly built aircraft. America's aviation industry was practically killed off, and aviation innovation became a European triumph during the 1920s and 1930s. During World War II, the Germans made a number of aeronautical advances such as the 35-degree swept wing and leading-edge slats to improve low-speed handing characteristics, while the British and the Germans simultaneously, yet separately, developed their own versions of the jet engine.

Although caught behind the technology curve when World War II started, by 1943 the United States was out-producing the Axis powers as well as developing and building large numbers of new aircraft. America's ability to mass-produce aircraft enabled the Allies to dominate the sky in both numbers of aircraft as well as control of the air space. By war's end, America had delivered 18,188 Consolidated B-24 Liberators, 14,819 North American Aviation P-51 Mustangs, 12,731 Boeing B-17 Flying Fortresses, 12,571 Vought F4U Corsairs, and the list goes on and on. In total, from January 1940 to the day the Japanese surrendered in August 1945, more than 300,000 aircraft were built in the United States at a cost of more than $43 billion.

In an effort to avoid repeating the great aviation surplus sell-off mistakes made after World War I, the U.S. government commissioned a number of studies on what to do with surplus aircraft, engines, ships, and vehicles. To address the issue of so many surplus aircraft, a survey was commissioned to determine how best to dispose of surplus aircraft and the component parts that make up a fighting aircraft. The project involved a B-24 Liberator, and was known as Project Herkimer—Air Service Command Project No. 41021. The project's intention was to determine the value of a war-weary bomber and the costs associated with extracting all of the component parts.

Project Herkimer was named after *Herkimer*, a B-24D Liberator, designed by Consolidated Aircraft Company and built at the company's Ft. Worth, Texas, assembly line. The aircraft was serial number 41-24245, and was accepted by the Army Air Forces on 28 November 1942. After post-delivery modifications, it was flown away from the factory on 19 December 1942. The aircraft was sent to Langley Field, Virginia, to patrol for submarines off the U.S. East Coast with the 18th Anti-Submarine Squadron. Then, on 19 May 1943, *Herkimer* was sent overseas under code GLEN A to the 12th Air Force in North Africa. From here the Liberator would bomb targets in the Mediterranean Theater as the Allied armies moved from North Africa to Sicily. On 18 November 1943, *Herkimer* returned stateside, was overhauled, and the now war-weary bomber was flown to Patterson Field, Ohio.

It was at Patterson Field where Project Herkimer began. Here, a team of Air Service Command mechanics neatly stripped *Herkimer* to pieces. Engines, instruments, radios, wiring, electric motors, and hydraulic reservoirs—everything that could come off the bomber did. While each piece was removed, the time to accomplish the task was logged to help determine the cost of salvaging the bomber. In all, Project Herkimer determined that it took 782.51 man-hours to reduce a B-24 bomber to 32,759 pounds of components that covered more than an acre when laid out. As a point of reference, it took Consolidated Aircraft 23,698 man-hours (10,938 direct and 12,760 indirect) to build a B-24D and it cost the government $236,347.09 for each bomber.

With *Herkimer* reduced to pounds of parts, representatives from industry were brought in to see what could be reused to make new industrial products and consumer goods. Upon inspection, most of the manufacturers' representatives declined the offer to use *Herkimer's* recycled parts as they preferred to "make new"

in order to guarantee that the products they produced would work the first time, every time. Unable to find a buyer for the parts, the government was faced with what to do with more than 33,000 surplus war machines.

To sort out the surplus problem, the Army Air Forces divided storage fields into those with obsolete aircraft and those holding the weapons of war that could be recalled to duty in times of conflict. Obsolete aircraft went to

From the end of World War II until the summer of 1948, storage yards across the country were filled with obsolete fighters and bombers. Here factory-fresh Lockheed P-38 Lightnings sit in the Arizona sun with fields of B-24 Liberator bombers. In the distance are groups of B-17s, B-25s, new B-32s, and other implements of the air war. These aircraft sit at Kingman, Arizona, along Route 66 in the summer of 1947. By summer of the following year they had been converted to aluminum ingots and resold to make new consumer goods. **(Veronico Collection)**

places like Kingman, Arizona; Walnut-Ridge, Arkansas; Cal-Aero Field near Ontario, California; Albuquerque, New Mexico; and Clinton and Altus, Oklahoma—28 fields in all. In June 1946, the Reconstruction Finance Corporation (RFC), the government's agency charged with disposing of surplus property, placed the aircraft sitting at the six fields named above up for auction—a total of 20,703 aircraft.

The Wunderlich Contracting Company of Jefferson City, Missouri, won the bid for the aircraft at Kingman. The company paid $2.78 million for the privilege of reducing 5,483 aircraft to aluminum ingots. When the U.S. government put the airplanes up for sale it wanted them gone. To that end, Wunderlich Contracting was given 18 months to clear the field.

Wunderlich's Kingman scrapping operation recovered 45.7 million pounds of aluminum from aircraft airframes, 20.9 million pounds of steel, 6.2 million pounds of aluminum from engines, and 4.8 million pounds of aluminum propellers. In addition, by draining the fuel and oil tanks, as well as the engine sumps, Wunderlich Contracting recovered an additional 1.575 million gallons of aviation gasoline and 255,782 gallons of oil. Wunderlich Contracting is estimated to have sold the scrap of its 5,483 aircraft for $7.5 million (gross income). By the middle of 1948, the thousands of surplus, war-weary bombers left over from World War II had met

their fate with the scrapper's torch and had been completely eliminated. The metal recovered from these war machines was returned to the American economy and became pots and pans as well as 1948 Fords, Buicks, and Chevrolets.

While the obsolete aircraft were being disposed of, a strategic reserve of combat aircraft was established at Pyote, Texas, and Davis-Monthan Army Air Field, outside of Tucson, Arizona. On these fields were parked fleets of C-47 Skytrain transports, long-range bombers such as the Boeing B-29 Stratofortress, and America's newest light bomber, the Douglas A-26 Invader. In addition to the two storage facilities, six storage depots were formed at Hill Air Force Base, Ogden, Utah; Tinker AFB, Oklahoma City, Oklahoma; Kelly AFB, San Antonio, Texas; Norton AFB, San Bernardino, California; McClellan AFB, Sacramento, California; and the Warner Robins Air Materiel Area, Warner, Georgia.

Davis-Monthan Army Air Field was a plot of arid land in the Sonoran Desert south of Tucson, having a climate that is ideal for storing aircraft outdoors. During the war, the base's outstanding weather enabled thousands of four-engine B-24 bomber crews to fly countless hours learning to become cohesive combat crews before being sent to fight in Europe or the Pacific.

Storage operations at Davis-Monthan were consolidated under the 4105th AAF Base Unit (Aircraft Storage), part of the Second Air

Force. As 1946 drew to a close, more than 690 B-29s and 241 C-47s were parked at Davis-Monthan in anticipation of a call to duty that lay five years in the future. Additionally, Davis-Monthan was storing 30 aircraft that were slated to form the nucleus of a future U.S. Air Force museum. The museum collection included the sole Douglas B-19, Wendell Wilkie's C-87, a Consolidated Vultee B-32 Dominator, the Beech XC-38 Destroyer equipped with a 75mm cannon, and an XCG-17 glider version of the Douglas C-47. However, only the B-24D *Strawberry Bitch*, the B-29s *Enola Gay* and *Bockscar*, a German Ju-88, and President Franklin D. Roosevelt's C-54 "Sacred Cow" were saved.

In order to properly manage its strategic reserve of aircraft, the Air Force developed a storage classification system. First the aircraft were organized into classes by storage type (Class I, strategic reserve; Class II, operational reserve; Class III, excess; and Class IV, surplus). Aircraft within those groups were stored according to the type of preservation required (Type A, short term—ready to fly within 72 hours; Type B, indefinite temporary storage—available for operations within seven days; Type C, extended storage; and Type D, storage of temporarily grounded aircraft).

To preserve the stored bombers and fighters from deterioration while parked in the elements, the Air Force then began investigating methods to keep the airplanes in top

Developed as a strategic reserve, the storage center at Davis-Monthan was stocked with B-29 bombers and C-47 transports. When this May 1946 aerial photograph was taken, there were more than 600 Superfortresses and 200 C-47s, plus 30 aircraft that were being stored for a future Air Force museum collection. **(Courtesy AMARG)**

B-29 44-70108, Sweet Thing, *was assigned to the 678th Bomb Squadron of the 444th Bomb Wing. The 444th was the first B-29 combat group established during World War II, flying from bases in India. The unit later operated against targets in Japan from its base at Tinian.* Sweet Thing *is seen in storage at Davis-Monthan in 1946, and was eventually reclaimed at Tinker AFB, Oklahoma, in July 1954. (R. F. Schirmer/American Aviation Historical Society)*

Tests of various cocooning materials were undertaken at the Warner Robins Air Materiel Area, Georgia, in July 1946. Air Materiel Command believed it could save nearly $6 million per year in maintenance costs by cocooning its fleet of B-29s. (National Archives)

All of the aircraft's openings, including the engine cowlings, were covered with tape before the cocooning sealant was applied. Tape was used to build up the area from the cowling nose bowl to the propeller spinner. Today's aircraft cocooning has been refined to a science and the amount of scaffolding, jacks, and hoses seen in this photo has been virtually eliminated. (R. F. Schirmer/American Aviation Historical Society)

This Boeing-Wichita-built Superfortress, serial number 44-69909, was the first to undergo the cocooning procedure at Warner Robins and was photographed on 11 July 1946. Nine months after the cocoons were applied, a number of the Superfortresses were opened and found to be in excellent condition. (National Archives)

The cocoon consisted of a yellow coat of Insulmastic sealant followed by a coat with red pigment. Varying the colors ensured a readily visible way to determine if both coats had been fully applied. This B-29 at Davis-Monthan is receiving its second coat, the red being applied from the highest point on the tail and working down toward the fuselage. The red and yellow coats were followed by a black Gilsonite (a natural, resinous, petroleum product) layer, then a white Gilsonite coating to reflect the sun. (R. F. Schirmer/American Aviation Historical Society)

condition. Yes, they would need some preparation when recalled to active duty, but developing an adequate preservation method would keep this maintenance to a minimum.

The Army Air Force's Air Materiel Command (AMC), Engineering Division, oversaw the development of a cocooning method for the more than 1,000 B-29 atomic bombers that were to be kept in reserve. In July 1946, the project got underway at Warner Robins AAF Base with the Fort Pitt Packaging Company and the J.I. Hass Company supplying labor for the cocooning efforts while the cocooning specifications and materials were supplied by AMC.

To cocoon a B-29 bomber, contractors installed 1,300 pounds of silica gel desiccant and humidity indicators in the aircraft and covered all openings with tape, which was followed by red and yellow layers of sprayed-on plastic. A black Gilsonite (asphalt-based) covering, known as Insulmastic, was applied over the plastic, which was finally sealed with an aluminum-colored paint. Clear plastic windows were left in the cocoon to allow the aircraft's interior to be monitored.

Nine months after the cocooning project was initiated, one of the B-29s was opened for inspection and found to be in excellent condition. However, materials used for cocooning had suffered, as sprayed-on plastic layers expanded and contracted at greater rates than Gilsonite. New cocooning materials have been developed as technology improved.

While the Boeing bombers and Douglas transports were being neatly parked and preserved on the Sonoran Desert's clay soil, the U.S. Army's aviation arm was being transformed by President Truman's Executive Order 9877, which established the U.S. Air Force as an independent branch of the armed forces on 18 September 1947.

During the early months of 1948, the Cold War began heating up. To ensure there were enough frontline aircraft available, 100 Boeing B-29s were sent through the Gem modification program, many of which were drawn from strategic reserve stocks. The Gem modifications included "Saddletree" upgrades to enable the Superfortress to carry nuclear weapons, as well as fitting the bombers with new upgraded electronics, radar systems, and communications equipment. On 28 August 1948, the 4105th was redesignated the 3040th Aircraft Storage Depot and aircraft reclamation and salvage were added to the unit's mission.

The value of maintaining a strategic reserve of aircraft was demonstrated in the summer and fall of 1950. On 26 June of that year, the communist North Korean Army invaded South Korea. As U.S. forces responded, calls came in for additional transport aircraft and more parts for B-29 bombers. The 3040th Aircraft Storage Depot stripped 27 B-29s at Davis-Monthan for spare parts to maintain the flying Superfortress fleet. Each aircraft returned between $270,000 and $350,000 worth of parts to the inventory. An additional 173 B-29s parked at Pyote and Warner Robins Air Force Base, Georgia, were reduced to spares to aid in the war effort.

The end of the Korean conflict saw a reverse tide of aircraft. In the six months after the end of the Korean War, from June to December 1953, more than 770 aircraft were delivered to the 3040th Aircraft Storage Depot. With this rising tide, additional parking space was required and 480 acres adjoining the air base were acquired.

The value of a strategic aircraft reserve and the ability to draw parts from it was not lost on Air Force planners, and on 21 May 1954, the 3040th was designated as the Air Force's aircraft storage facility within the United States. The aircraft inventory at Pyote was sent to the smelter, thus ensuring the 3040th Aircraft Storage Depot's role in managing the Air Force's strategic aircraft reserve. On 1 June 1956, the 3040th became the Arizona Aircraft Storage Branch (AASB), a component of the San Bernardino Air Materiel Area.

On 1 August 1959, the AASB became the 2704th Air Force Aircraft Storage and Disposition Group (later AF Storage and Disposition Group) under AMC, which was headquartered at Wright-Patterson AFB, Ohio. Eight months later, on 1 April 1961, AMC was separated into two commands: Air Force Logistics Command (AFLC) and Air Force Systems

For a time, aircraft that were to form the nucleus of the Air Force's future museum were stored at Davis-Monthan. It is extremely rare to have not only an aerial view of this collection but a photograph in color as well. Here is the Boeing B-29 Enola Gay *sitting in the front row (closest to the camera with the circle "R" insignia on its tail), and the B-29* Bockscar *sitting in the fourth row between a B-32 and the B-24* Strawberry Bitch. *These two B-29s were the world's first and only aircraft to ever drop nuclear weapons in time of war. (Harry Gann via Pima Air & Space Museum)*

Command (AFSC); the 2704th became a subordinate command of AFLC.

To facilitate parts recycling, a new $590,000 reclamation shelter was completed in 1962. This 918-foot-long shelter placed 180,072 square feet of work space in the shade, enabling an aircraft to be parked under it, have all necessary parts removed, cleaned, packaged, and shipped out, and the aircraft returned to storage. The area around the shelter, 650,000 square feet, was graded, packed, and seal coated to accommodate aircraft waiting their turn at reclamation.

Five years later, in September 1964, the Department of Defense saw the need to eliminate many of the redundant tasks being accomplished by both the Air Force and the U.S. Navy. Aircraft storage was one of those areas identified. While the Air Force had been storing its aircraft at Davis-Monthan AFB, the Navy (including the Marines and Coast Guard) had located its long-term storage at Litchfield Park, 150 miles to the northwest near Phoenix, Arizona. With the consolidation, the U.S. Army added its inventory to the aircraft stored at Davis-Monthan AFB as well.

Along with the addition of Army, Navy, Marines, and Coast Guard aircraft came a name change. On 1 February 1965, the storage activity at Davis-Monthan AFB was redesignated the Military Aircraft Storage and Disposition Center, or MASDC, to provide a "single operation for processing and maintaining aircraft in storage; preparation of aircraft for one-time flight, transfer, or inspection; reclamation of aircraft/aircraft engines and components for inventory replenishment and/or special projects; processing of aircraft/aircraft engines and residue for disposal; administration of sales and/or service contracts with foreign governments, other governmental agencies, and commercial contractors; and perform field level maintenance on selected aircraft systems and components."

During the Vietnam War, aircraft and parts were provided for the war effort. For example, when the B-52Bs were retired from service, they were maintained in storage instead of being immediately scrapped. When B-52 engines were needed on Guam as replacements for aircraft serving in combat, J57-29 turbojet engines were removed and trucked to March AFB in Riverside, California, then airlifted to the island base. In 1967, 266 B-52 engines worth $56,921,974 were removed from stored B-52s and sent to the combat theater.

After Vietnam, MASDC continued to serve as a strategic reserve during the Cold War. By

Enola Gay in storage at Davis-Monthan. Note the aircraft's lack of upper and lower turrets, a weight-reduction effort to enable the bomber to carry nuclear weapons. Having dropped the first atomic bomb on the Japanese city of Hiroshima on 6 August 1945, this aircraft holds a significant place in American aviation history and is now on display at the Smithsonian Institution's National Air and Space Museum's Steven F. Udvar-Hazy Center in Chantilly, Virginia. (U.S. Air Force via Wayne Gomes)

Bockscar, a Glenn L. Martin-built B-29, serial number 44-27297, was named for its pilot Frederick C. Bock. This Superfortress dropped the world's second atomic bomb on the city of Nagasaki on 9 August 1945, which ultimately led to the end of the war in the Pacific. Bockscar was sent to Davis-Monthan for storage in September 1946 and sat until it made its last flight in September 1961 when the historic bomber was flown to the National Museum of the U.S. Air Force at Wright-Patterson AFB, Ohio.

When communist North Korean forces crossed into South Korea on 25 June 1950, the United States and United Nations were not going to allow such aggression to go unchecked. Naval aircraft onboard carriers were quickly dispatched to help stem the North Korean tide threatening to wipe out the South. B-29s based in the area were called to action, and Superfortresses held in strategic reserve were removed from storage to equip new bomb groups. Cocooning material is removed from a B-29 at Davis-Monthan in this September 1950 view of a Superfortress being returned to service. (Veronico collection)

Aerial view of Davis-Monthan Air Force Base in early 1950 showing the B-29s parked together, the majority of them cocooned. Three-quarters of these Super-fortresses were removed to meet the Strategic Air Command's needs during the Korean War. (National Archives)

1985, a name change was needed in an effort to inform the American taxpayers of the tremendous value Davis-Monthan's storage activities played, not only in returning millions of dollars worth of parts and aircraft to the inventory, but to show the industrial importance to its southern Arizona neighbors. MASDC became the Aerospace Maintenance and Regeneration Center (AMARC) serving the armed forces through the Gulf War, Kosovo, Bosnia, and, in the wake of the terrorist attacks on the United States, in support of Operation Iraqi Freedom and Operation Enduring Freedom in Afghanistan. In May 2007, AMARC was transferred under the control of the 309th Maintenance Wing, Hill AFB, Utah, to become the 309th Aerospace Maintenance and Regeneration Group (309 AMARG). In addition to aircraft storage and parts reclamation, 309 AMARG restores aircraft to flying condition for its military customers, depot-level maintenance, and aircraft disposal.

Today 309 AMARG stores more than 4,200 aircraft that cost the taxpayers more than $35 billion when originally purchased. Depot-level maintenance is performed on a variety of aircraft, and one of its current maintenance programs is a service life extension of the A-10 Thunderbolt II. In addition to the Air Force, Navy, Marines, and Coast Guard, NASA and other government agencies store aircraft with 309 AMARG and use the unit's services to keep their aircraft in the air.

America's first Mach 2 strategic bomber, the Convair B-58 Hustler, was one of the big fleets that met its end at Davis-Monthan. This aircraft, serial number 61-2079, last flew with the 305th Bomb Wing and was christened The Thumper. It is wearing storage center inventory number BQ039 and is seen being prepared for storage shortly after its 14 December 1969, arrival in the desert. (AMARG photo)

A Coast Guard Consolidated P4Y-2G, BuNo. 66320, sits among rows of Skyraiders and TV-2 Shooting Stars at the Navy storage facility in April 1958. The U.S. Navy, Marines, and Coast Guard stored their aircraft at Litchfield Park, Arizona, west of Phoenix, from the end of World War II through September 1964, when redundant, cross-service operations were eliminated. Under this program, all military services combined their storage activities at Davis-Monthan. (Brian R. Baker)

Five of the 14 C-74s built by Douglas at the company's Long Beach, California, assembly plant were held as a strategic airlift reserve at Davis-Monthan. The type was powered by four Pratt & Whitney R-4360-27 or -49 engines rated at 3,000 horsepower each. In the original-configuration cockpit, C-74 pilots sat under separate canopies giving the aircraft a rather "bug-eyed" look, although later versions had the airliner-type cockpit and windshield shown here. Many of the C-74s, including this aircraft, flew in the Berlin Airlift. Although a few were sold as surplus and entered the civilian market, this C-74 (42-65414) was scrapped. (Brian R. Baker)

In addition to storage, a number of unique tests are conducted on aircraft at the facility. Here a technician prepares a specially designed cannon to fire shrapnel into the engines of a B-52D Stratofortress aircraft at the Military Aircraft Storage and Disposition Center (MASDC). Damage caused by the cannon will be repaired by members of the 2954th Combat Logistics Support Squadron during the aircraft battle damage repair exercise NIGHT TRAIN '84. (U.S. Air Force/SSgt. John A. Pickett)

The battle damage infliction gun used to simulate anti-aircraft damage is positioned under the wing of a B-52 Stratofortress during Exercise NIGHT TRAIN/GLOBAL SHIELD 1984. (U.S. Air Force/TSgt. Rob Marshall)

This gaggle of Lockheed T-33s was delivered to storage in 1980 from the U.S. Air Force. They were subsequently transferred to the U.S. Navy for use in the QT-33 drone program. Nearest the camera (wearing inventory number TCB92) is 52-9757 (U.S. Navy BuNo. 156131). The QT-33 drone program was dropped in favor of higher performance drone aircraft such as the QF-100, QF-106, and QF-4. (Karen B. Haack)

A-4s, F-4s, and F-106s being removed from storage in January 1990. F-106A 56-0457, 50-0035, and F-106B 57-2547 were subsequently converted to QF-106 drones, while A-4M BuNo. 160042, formerly of Marine Attack Squadron 322, is being prepared for its new owners, the Argentine Navy. Once in Argentina, the aircraft was redesignated an A-4AR and given serial number C-930. (Karen B. Haack)

Every military aircraft type in the U.S. inventory eventually passes through AMARG, including the most dominant air-superiority fighter of the last quarter century, the F-15 Eagle. Four fully preserved Eagles await another call to duty, or to surrender parts to keep other aircraft flying. (Nicholas A. Veronico)

Douglas A-4 Skyhawks as far as the eye can see. These nimble fighters served as aggressor aircraft to train U.S. Navy pilots. A-4F BuNo. 155018 last flew with VF-126 and was flown to storage on 28 March 1994. (Nicholas A. Veronico)

The newest type of aircraft entered the AMARG fleet on 24 July 2008, when B-52H 61-0023 touched down at Davis-Monthan. The turbofan-powered H-model B-52s will be kept intact should they need to be recalled to active duty. **(AMARG)**

More than 90 Boeing B-52Gs sit in the AMARG storage yards. Here half a dozen Stratofortresses undergo parts reclamation in anticipation of their being cut into five sections in compliance with the Strategic Arms Reduction Treaty (START) agreement. Under the terms of the agreement, the bombers are cut into five pieces, and then left in place for 90 days to enable Russian satellites to verify their destruction. **(Nicholas A. Veronico)**

An aerial image of the 309th Aerospace Maintenance and Regeneration Group's (AMARG) vast storage fields located on the Davis-Monthan Air Force Base in Tucson, Arizona. AMARG is responsible for the storage and maintenance of aircraft for future redeployment, parts, or proper disposal following retirement by the military. Modern military aircraft from C-141s (lower) to F-111s (center) to B-1 Lancer bombers (left center) can be seen in this aerial view. (U.S. Navy photo by Photographer's Mate 3rd Class Shannon R. Smith)

AIRCRAFT STORAGE AND DISPOSAL

Fairchild-Republic A-10 79-0139 arrived at AMARG on 19 January 2000, to undergo the A-10 service life extension program (SLEP) upgrades. This aircraft was assigned AMARG inventory number AC-0199 and is seen here undergoing the induction process before work can begin. Once the SLEP was complete, 79-0139 returned to service with the 23rd Fighter Group at Pope AFB, North Carolina, on 14 April 2000. (Nicholas A. Veronico)

AMARG is responsible for maintaining aircraft from all branches of the U.S. armed forces—Air Force, Army, Coast Guard, Navy, and Marine Corps, and serves a number of federal agencies as well—Customs and Border Patrol, State Department, NASA, and the Smithsonian Institution. AMARG also maintains aircraft for foreign governments, such as the F-111s held in storage for the Australian Air Force, and U.S. aircraft sold through various foreign military sales efforts often come from storage stocks to fulfill such orders.

Organizationally, AMARG is comprised of four squadrons: the 576th Aerospace Maintenance and Regeneration Squadron, which is responsible for repairing aircraft and returning aircraft to the active fleet; the 577th Commodities Reclamation Squadron, which manages all parts and aircraft subassemblies from removal to inspection and repair; the 578th Storage and Disposal Squadron, which is responsible for storage and removal of aircraft and missiles from the storage inventory; and the 309th Support Squadron, which packs and ships aircraft and parts.

Prior to arrival, the aircraft's controlling agency has determined an aircraft's or rotorcraft's fate, such as what level of preservation is required, if the aircraft or its type is anticipated to be recalled to service, or if there are any particular parts or subassemblies that need to be removed and sent to a depot-level overhaul program to keep other aircraft flying in the fleet. This information is given to AMARG's 578th Storage and Disposal Squadron, which then determines what level of preservation is required. There are five preservation levels:

- Type 1000 denotes long-term storage where the aircraft should be maintained in an intact condition with the potential of being recalled to active service.
- Type 1500 represents long-term storage of Navy aircraft that are not expected to return to service due to having operated in a salt-air environment. Their subassemblies and other internal parts, however, may be required in the future.
- Type 2000 signifies aircraft in a programmed parts reclamation storage where aircraft are expected to yield as many parts as possible to keep others in flying condition. Removed parts are cleaned, tested, packaged, and shipped to repair depots around the world.
- Type 3000 denotes an aircraft in flyable hold storage, and is often applied to aircraft awaiting transfer to a foreign government.
- Type 4000 storage signifies an aircraft that has had every useable part reclaimed and is ready to be recycled.

When an aircraft arrives for storage, it lands on the Davis-Monthan AFB runways, and then taxies to the AMARG facility. Once the crew deplanes and any farewell ceremonies have been completed, the aircraft's inventory number, also known as a Production Control Number (PCN—an eight letter/digit code in black spray paint), is applied. The aircraft then has any armament and ejection-seat charges removed. Completion of these items earns a green spray-painted cross on the nose of the port side that serves as a quick visual identifier to any AMARG employee that all explosives and armament have been removed.

Next a detailed inventory of the aircraft and its contents is made. Any classified items are secured, and a detailed inspection is

Ski-equipped LC-130R Bureau Number (BuNo.) 160741 sat in storage for three years before being recalled to active duty. On 30 March 2000, this aircraft was flown to Waco, Texas, and upgraded to LC-130H configuration. It subsequently returned to service with the National Science Foundation flying supplies from New Zealand to McMurdo Station, Antarctica. The LC-130Hs can haul more than 26,800 pounds of equipment and passengers from the McMurdo base to the South Pole and back without refueling. (Ron Strong)

In 2003, scientists at NASA Ames Research Center in Mountain View, California, determined that it needed a method to showcase a number of aviation human-factors-related technologies. The intent was to develop a display where dignitaries and the general public could sit in an aircraft cockpit and interact with the technologies in a realistic environment.

Since the P-3 was originally designed as the Lockheed Electra airliner and NASA Ames is located next to the former NAS Moffett Field, an ex-P-3 base, the Electra-based Orion was a great fit. Plans called for the P-3's steam gauges to be replaced with an all-glass instrument panel, a heads-up display, and other accommodations that would best showcase new NASA human-factors aviation technologies.

Transferring the cockpit between the Navy and NASA was just a matter of paperwork, and there was no acquisition cost to the space agency. Even though the cockpit was free, NASA would have to reimburse the Navy for removal and transportation costs.

NASA sent a representative to AMARG to work with Navy specialists at the storage facility to select an aircraft best suited for the conversion. The aircraft selected was TP-3A, BuNo. 151370, which was originally delivered to the U.S. Navy by Lockheed on 4 June 1964. The four-engine patrol aircraft then served with Patrol Squadron 16 (VP-16), VP-8, VP-92, VP-94, and flew its last tour with VP-30. On 27 April 1995, the aircraft was flown to AMARG for storage.

In 2003, the cockpit was removed and the rest of the aircraft was sealed to provide parts for other P-3s still in the fleet. The cockpit arrived at NASA Ames in January 2004, where clean-up work began immediately. Subsequently, NASA's funding for the project was cut and the cockpit was transferred to the Moffett Field Museum where it has been painstakingly restored by museum staff. The cockpit now serves as an educational tool and a tribute to the thousands of P-3 crews who passed through Moffett Field.

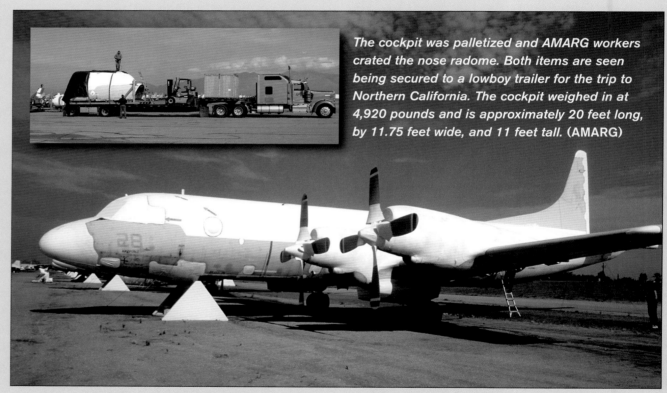

The cockpit was palletized and AMARG workers crated the nose radome. Both items are seen being secured to a lowboy trailer for the trip to Northern California. The cockpit weighed in at 4,920 pounds and is approximately 20 feet long, by 11.75 feet wide, and 11 feet tall. **(AMARG)**

Lockheed TP-3A BuNo. 151370 was delivered to the Navy in June 1964. The aircraft was flown to storage in April 1995. By 2003, it was being inspected to see if the cockpit could serve NASA as a technology demonstrator. **(Nicholas A. Veronico)**

Cribbing has been added behind the bomb bay to secure the aircraft once the cockpit is removed. Even with protective coating, the P-3's clean lines reveal the airplane's commercial airliner roots of Lockheed's classic turboprop Electra from 1959. (AMARG)

A chalk line indicates where the saw cuts should be made. Here the line is below the cabin floor. Rectangular openings seen in the lower fuselage were covered by access hatches when this P-3 was flying as an operational aircraft. (AMARG)

The removal process was done by hand, with an AMARG employee using a gasoline-powered saw to cut through the aluminum structure. Note the spray-painted AMARG inventory number (AN2P0161) above the chalk line. (AMARG)

At the end of the first day, the section below the cockpit that once held the nose landing gear has been removed and the scrap metal placed in a can behind the aircraft. This scrap will be recycled and the proceeds returned to the government. (AMARG)

The cockpit was delivered to NASA Ames on 16 January 2004. Upon delivery the cockpit was moved into NASA's historic Hangar 211 at Moffett Federal Airfield where clean-up work was begun. (Nicholas A. Veronico)

The interior was relatively complete when it arrived at NASA for conversion to a technology demonstrator. Lockheed also used this basic cockpit layout for its turboprop Electra airliner and C-130 Hercules cargo transport. (Nicholas A. Veronico)

accomplished. Completion of this task earns a gold spray-painted number "7" above or near the green cross. Next the fuel system is drained and the engine preserved. The hydraulic system is serviced and the aircraft is thoroughly washed and sprayed with a corrosion inhibitor.

Then the craft is towed to the shelter area to begin the sealing process. All openings on the upper sides of the aircraft are taped, leaving the lower portion open for air circulation. Engine inlets and exhausts are covered and then the first of two coats of plastic "spraylat" are applied. The first layer is black and the top layer is white to reflect sunlight. The combination of open lower areas with spraylat applied to canopies and upper surfaces allows an aircraft's interior to maintain a temperature within 15 to 20 degrees of the outside air temperature. Every six months after arrival, aircraft are inspected to ensure that the elements have not damaged the spraylat and, after four years, the planes are recycled through the preservation process.

Aircraft depart AMARG in one of two ways: under their own power or on a truck. Over the years, it has been estimated that more than 25 percent of all aircraft in storage have flown out for further service. AMARG technicians prepare the aircraft for flight by withdrawing the plane from storage, inspecting and repairing or overhauling systems, and modifying an aircraft to current standards by meeting Time Compliance Technical Orders. Many aircraft or subassemblies, such as nose sections or fuselages slated for use as trainers, are trucked from the center.

To commemorate the sacrifices of this nation's service men and women, obsolete combat aircraft and missiles are made available for loan or gift to museums, qualifying municipalities, or veterans' groups such as the American Legion, Veterans of Foreign Wars, and Disabled American Veterans. AMARG supervises this program by monitoring aircraft loan requests, verifying donation eligibility, and monitoring the removal of aircraft from storage. Donation aircraft are offered on an "as-is, where-is" basis, and each receiving organization must bear the full cost to disassemble, transport, and display an aircraft within 90 days. Once an aircraft has been placed on display, a yearly photographic survey is made to ensure it is being

The maintenance shelter is seen with a pair of KC-97s and eight T-33s awaiting attention on the ramp. In the lower right, two rows of F-86 Sabres are in the queue for processing. Note the large number of C-119s and B-47s in storage to the left. (AMARG)

maintained properly and protected from vandalism and decay.

Recently, to support a T-38 fleet-wide inspection and upgrade, AMARG crews removed more than 3,500 parts from Talons in storage. The parts were packed and shipped to the Ogden Air Logistics Center at Hill AFB, Utah, where the T-38s were being inspected with a special look at the fleet's flight control system. Using the AMARG-supplied parts the flight control systems were inspected and repaired as necessary. The T-38 reclamation effort was just one task during fiscal year 2008, which saw AMARG reclaim and ship 17,341 parts worth more than $500.2 million.

AMARG's 576th Aerospace Maintenance and Regeneration Squadron is supporting the A-10 service life extension program (SLEP), which includes strengthening the fighter's wings, repairing any corrosion around internal wing fuel tanks, and adding spar straps to increase the wing's strength. The SLEP increases the A-10's life span from 8,000 flying hours to 16,000.

The squadron is also removing and preparing a large number of F-4s for drone conversion as part of the Air Combat Command's Full Scale Aerial Target Program (FSAT). It is anticipated that the F-16 will be the next-FSAT-generation airframe in the program, and AMARG would play a leading role in delivering surplus Fighting Falcons to the drone conversion contractors.

On 18 March 2008, a number of aircraft arrived for storage including this two-seat McDonnell Douglas F-15B, serial number 76-0125. This Eagle last saw service with the 125th Fighter Wing, Florida ANG, operating at the NORAD Air Defense Alert site at Homestead Air Reserve Base. Earlier in its career, 76-0125 had flown with the 525th Tactical Fighter Squadron at Bitburg, Germany. Note that this aircraft lacks the green AMARG cross, which signifies that this F-15's explosives, such as ejection seats, remain active. (Ron Strong)

Recently removed from storage and giving up parts are McDonnell Douglas RF-4C serial number 68-0582 last flown by the 91st Tactical Reconnaissance Squadron (TRS) 67th Tactical Reconnaissance Wing from Bergstrom AFB, Texas, and RF-4C serial number 66-0475, 196th TRS of the California Air National Guard. (Ron Strong)

Ex-Maine Air National Guard KC-135 serial number 57-1471 arrived at AMARG on 17 March 2008. The aircraft has not yet undergone the intake process. (Ron Strong)

When Marine Air Refueling and Transport Squadron 152 (VMGR-152) received its new Lockheed Martin KC-130Js in June 2007, everyone knew that the older, dependable KC-130Fs the squadron flew would soon be retired. VMGR-152, based at Okinawa, Japan, flew its last—and the Marine Corps' first delivered—KC-130F BuNo. 147573 to AMARG for storage on 27 February 2008. This KC-130F was acquired by the Marine Corps in 1961, and had flown more than 28,000 hours by the time it was retired. Note that the crew has autographed the aircraft. Many times personal notes or poems are written by departing crews. It should be noted that VMGR-152 commanding officer Lt. Col. Dwight Neeley flew the Blue Angels C-130 Fat Albert for the team from 1998 to 2000. (Ron Strong)

On the wash rack, a line of Phantoms and a ski-equipped C-130 await attention from the AMARG preservation crews. From left: F-4E 71-0238 from the 3rd Tactical Fighter Wing, RF-4C 69-0362 wearing the markings of its last operator (4485th Test Squadron at Eglin AFB, Florida), F-4E 71-1073 also from the 3rd Tactical Fighter Wing with the PN "3TFS" tail markings, and ski-equipped LC-130R (Air Force serial 76-3302, BuNo. 160741) from VXE-6. The LC-130R was flown from storage and upgraded at Waco, Texas, and subsequently returned to servicing the Antarctic station with the 139th Air Wing of the New York ANG. (Nicholas A. Veronico)

F-4E 74-1650 is seen on the wash rack undergoing the represervation process in March 2008. This Phantom was flown to storage on 8 April 1991, having last flown with the 21st Tactical Fighter Training Squadron, 35th Tactical Fighter Wing at George AFB, California. The 35th Tactical Fighter Wing played a large role in Operation Desert Storm flying 3,072 combat missions of 10,318.5 hours. (Ron Strong)

F-16A serial number 81-0806 arrived at AMARG on 7 March 2008, and quickly entered the preservation process. All of the aircraft's skin openings have been taped over and plastic has been applied to bridge all large openings and areas requiring additional protection. Spraylat will be applied next. Once the intake process has been completed, the aircraft will be towed to its desert parking place. (Ron Strong)

McDonnell Douglas F-4G 69-7289, a former Wild Weasel surface-to-air defense suppression fighter, was retired after the 1991 Gulf War and sat in storage for eight years. In 2000, the aircraft was recalled for duty as an aerial drone. It was removed from storage and flown to BAE Systems/Flight Systems' facility at Mojave, California, where it was converted into a QF-4G drone. (Nicholas A. Veronico)

Rainy day F-4Es—one intact, one pickled. F-4E 72-0159 first flew on 23 April 1973, and last served with the 21st Tactical Fighter Training Squadron, 35th Tactical Fighter Wing at George AFB, California, before arriving for storage at AMARG on 26 April 1991. Shortly after this photo was taken, 72-0159 was flown on 29 June 2004, to BAE Systems at Mojave, California, and converted to an aerial target drone. As a QF-4E, the aircraft was given a new serial, AF271, and flown to Tyndall AFB, Florida, where it joined the 82nd Aerial Target Squadron. The cost to convert an F-4 to QF-4 configuration is approximately $800,000. (Nicholas A. Veronico)

These supersonic Convair F-106A Delta Darts are being prepared to fly away to become QF-106A target drones. As the backbone of the U.S. Air Force Air Defense Command, the F-106 offered Mach 2 performance and could launch nuclear-tipped anti-aircraft missiles. (Karen B. Haack)

The Douglas TA-4J was phased out of service in June 1998 at NAS Pensacola, Florida, having been replaced by the McDonnell Douglas T-45A/C Goshawk. TA-4J BuNo. 156941 arrived at AMARG from Training Wing 1 on 15 September 1999. (Nicholas A. Veronico)

F-16A serial number 83-1072, 170th Fighter Squadron, Illinois Air National Guard, entered storage on 17 October 1994. More than 400 of the type are now in storage and it is anticipated that these will soon be converted into high-speed target drones. (Nicholas A. Veronico)

The second layer of spraylat is being applied to this ex-Michigan Air National Guard F-16 in the shade of the maintenance shelter. (Ron Strong)

An AMARG maintenance crew in the final stages of replacing a KC-130 main gear wheel shortly after the aircraft arrived for storage, but before undergoing the spraylat process. (Ron Strong)

RF-4C serial number 68-0571 is supplying parts to keep drone QF-4s in flight. After hours of work, 68-0571 has yielded a cart full of stores pylons and hydraulic actuators. (Ron Strong)

Lockheed C-130E serial number 64-0538 arrived at AMARG on 7 February 2007, having last flown with the 314th Airlift Wing from Little Rock AFB, Arkansas. The C-130E is seen having its spraylat updated in May 2008. (Ron Strong)

Two test aircraft lead these rows of McDonnell Douglas F/A-18A Hornets. F/A-18A BuNo. 161715 (left) last served with the Naval Fighter Weapons School, or Top Gun, at NAS Miramar, California, before being retired on 21 April 1995. In 1996, the school was moved to NAS Fallon, Nevada. BuNo. 161720 (right) was last flown with the Naval Air Warfare Center—Weapons Division at NAS China Lake, California. Both Hornets remain in the AMARG inventory. (Nicholas A. Veronico)

This bagged RF-4C shows both the aircraft serial number (68-0574) and its AMARG inventory number (AAFP677) on the nose with a series of storage types and inspection dates stenciled near the engine intake. Note that this Phantom still retains its centerline weapons pylon. (Ron Strong)

Two U.S. Marine Corps F-4Es are receiving the attentions of AMARG staff. AMARG inventory number 8F0335 (left) corresponds to 74-1055, which was removed from storage and flown to BAE Systems at Mojave, California, for conversion into a QF-4E drone. Inventory number 8F0336 (right) is F-4E 74-1045, which is donating parts to keep other QF-4Es flying. (Ron Strong)

Blue Angels A-4 Skyhawk BuNo. 154179 sits on pallets ready for delivery to a waiting museum. This fighter arrived at AMARC on 13 February 1985, shortly after the Blue Angels transitioned into the F/A-18 Hornet. A-4s flew with the Blue Angels from 1974 to 1985 and the small but nimble fighter thrilled millions of spectators. Aircraft of the demonstration squadron were stripped of all combat gear and, after lightening the Skyhawk, the team had an 11,300-pound airplane with an engine that produced 11,400 pounds thrust. This improved thrust-to-weight ratio explains how the team performed so many outstanding maneuvers in the A-4. (Nicholas A. Veronico)

After six years of storage at AMARG, North American F-100 Super Sabre 56-3022 left for Mansfield, Ohio. The former supersonic fighter was put on display as a memorial to the men and women of the 178th Fighter Wing of the Ohio Air National Guard. (Nicholas A. Veronico)

The cockpit development fixture for building Northrop Grumman B-2 Stealth bombers is seen in storage in 2008. AMARG currently stores more than 350,000 line items of production tooling for the B-1, B-2, and A-10 on the east side of the facility. (Nicholas A. Veronico)

The U.S. Navy loaned EA-6B BuNo. 158542 to Grumman for a number of airframe structural upgrades under the Vehicle Enhancement Program, or VEP. The VEP modifications included a lengthened and strengthened vertical stabilizer, new slats and flaps, modified speed brakes, and airframe enhancements for improved airflow between the wing leading edge and cockpit. This aircraft was stored in September 1994 and returned to the Navy at Jacksonville, Florida, in April 1998. Most recently, 158542 was noted as serving with the Shadowhawks of VAQ-141 at NAS Whidbey Island, Washington. (Nicholas A. Veronico)

A pair of ex-German Panavia Tornadoes has been in storage since 1995. The aircraft were given to the National Museum of the U.S. Air Force, and it is antici-pated they will become museum pieces in the future. (Nicholas A. Veronico)

Boeing built a total of 1,831 727s, and this 727-100, N7004U, was the fifth one built. The three-engine jetliner was delivered to United Air Lines on 10 October 1963, and flew with the carrier until the Smithsonian Institution acquired it on 4 December 1991. The aircraft can be seen in storage on Celebrity Row. (Nicholas A. Veronico)

A winter storm approaches the aircraft of Celebrity Row. Pictured from left to right: T-2 Buckeye, T-39 Sabreliner, T-1A Seastar, T-46, T-33, T-38, T-34, NASA's Super Guppy, and an O-2. (Nicholas A. Veronico)

A number of Soviet-designed aircraft were imported into the United States during the 1980s to give American military pilots access and exposure to enemy equipment. When they became surplus to the military's needs, these aircraft were sent to AMARG for storage and subsequently transferred to the National Museum of the U.S. Air Force at Dayton, Ohio. On the left is a Polish-built version of the MiG-17, and on the right is an ex-Hungarian Air Force MiG-21. (Nicholas A. Veronico)

This unusual structure is the gondola from ZPG-3W, BuNo. 144243, the Navy's sole surviving post-World War II airborne early-warning blimp. It is reportedly being held for the National Museum of Naval Aviation in Pensacola, Florida. (Nicholas A. Veronico)

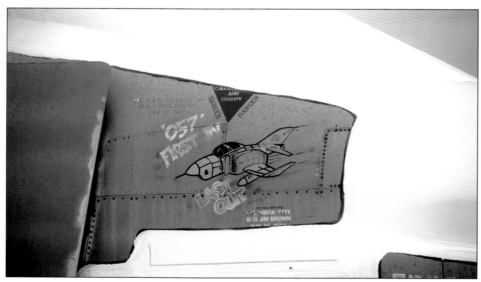

RF-4C 64-1057 wears a commemorative paint scheme to mark the retirement of the 117th Tactical Reconnaissance Wing, Alabama Air National Guard's use of the recon Phantom. Serial number 64-1057 was the first RF-4C to be received by the 117th and the last to be flown to the boneyard. The aircraft arrived on 26 May 1994, and has enjoyed a spot on Celebrity Row ever since. (Nicholas A. Veronico)

Boeing NKC-135A BuNo. 563596 was originally built for the U.S. Air Force as a KC-135A Stratotanker serial number 56-3596. It was subsequently modified to JKC-135A configuration and used to monitor the Soviet Union's nuclear program. The aircraft was then transferred to the U.S. Navy where its Air Force serial number (56-3596) was converted into the sea-service's Bureau of Aeronautics serial number (BuNo. 563596). The aircraft arrived for storage on 20 February 1996. (Nicholas A. Veronico)

Oceanographic Development Squadron Eight (VXE-8) aircraft were based at NAS Patuxent River, Maryland. VXE-8's UP-3As wore an orange-and-white high-visibility paint scheme and the tail title "World Traveler." Each was adorned with a cartoon character—in the case of BuNo. 150527 it was the Tasmanian Devil. Each aircraft had its anti-submarine gear removed and served as flying scientific platforms for the U.S. Navy and other government agencies. (Nicholas A. Veronico)

Celebrity Row resident Boeing C-22A 84-0193 was originally built as a 727-130, manufacturer's serial number 18363, for German airline Lufthansa. Christened Braunschweig, the trijet was delivered to the carrier on 1 April 1964. The aircraft was traded to Boeing for new equipment in 1974, and the 727 was subsequently acquired by the FAA and registered N78. The U.S. Air Force acquired the aircraft for personnel transport on 5 December 1983, and the aircraft flew in that role until 4 November 1991. (Nicholas A. Veronico)

YC-15A serial number 72-1875 (left) arrived at AMARC on 20 August 1979; the second prototype, 79-1876 (right), followed the next day. The first aircraft was delivered in McDonnell Douglas company colors and the second in tactical camouflage. The YC-15 and Boeing's YC-14 were designed to meet the Air Force's Advanced Medium Short Takeoff/Landing Transport (AMST) specification in the early 1970s. Each manufacturer developed a technology demonstrator aircraft that featured externally blown flaps using engine exhaust to produce lift that greatly improved takeoff and landing performance. Although neither aircraft was intended for production, McDonnell Douglas won the fly-off competition and incorporated much of the YC-15's technology into today's C-17 Globemaster III. (Nicholas A. Veronico)

Fairchild Republic's T-46 prototype (85-1596) was built as the intended replacement for the Air Force's primary jet trainer, the Cessna T-37, but never saw production. The aircraft was last operated by the 6512th Test Squadron at Edwards AFB, California, and was retired in May 1987. A second example of the T-46, 84-0493, is on display at the National Museum of the U.S. Air Force at Wright-Patterson AFB, Ohio. (Nicholas A. Veronico)

Seen at the end of the represervation process is Fairchild Republic A-10A serial number 77-0276 from the 10th Tactical Fighter Wing based at RAF Alconbury, United Kingdom. The unit began flying A-10s in 1987 and retired the type when the 10th TFW stood down on 27 March 1992. (Ron Strong)

A-10A serial number 77-0250 flew with the 10th Tactical Fighter Wing and still wears the name of its last pilot, Lt. Col. Magee. This aircraft arrived at AMARG shortly after the end of the Gulf War on 28 January 1992. (Ron Strong)

An unidentified A-10A is seen in the maintenance shelter during the service life extension program (SLEP). Attention is being paid to the aircraft's avionics at this time. (Nicholas A. Veronico)

A-10A 72-0241 has had its horizontal stabilizer, vertical tails, and wings removed, and the aircraft has been palletized. The aircraft awaits shipment to Ogden Air Logistics Center at Hill AFB, Utah, to undergo the A-10 service life extension program. (Ron Strong)

A-10A 75-0290 leads a row of stored Warthogs. This aircraft last flew with the 355th Fighter Wing at Davis-Monthan AFB, and was placed in storage on 2 October 1992. The aircraft is still in storage. (Nicholas A. Veronico)

Ex-Davis-Monthan AFB A-10A serial number 75-0261 was stripped of parts and sent to the air base's fire/rescue training facility. It was returned to storage in 2000. (Nicholas A. Veronico)

The helicopter came into its own as a military weapon during the Vietnam War, and has been used extensively in the ensuing years in the supply, search and rescue, medevac, scout, and gunship roles. Rows of Bell UH-1 Huey helicopters await the call to duty near a group of B-52Gs. (Nicholas A. Veronico)

Stored aircraft are also used as the backdrop for various military exercises. Here, pararescuemen and members of the Dutch Army rally near a C-141 Starlifter before searching for casualties during a joint mass casualty exercise 14 February 2006. The scenario involved a simulated shoot-down of the cargo plane by a missile. The pararescuemen are with the 48th Rescue Squadron. (U.S Air Force photo by Airman 1st Class Christina D. Ponte)

Members of a combat logistics support squadron wear nuclear, biological, and chemical (NBC) gear while repairing the wing of a B-52 Stratofortress aircraft during Exercise NIGHT TRAIN/GLOBAL SHIELD 1984. (U.S. Air Force/TSgt. Rob Marshall)

ALONG THE STORAGE ROWS

F-15A 76-0089 arrived at AMARG on 26 March 1992, having last operated with the 101st Fighter Squadron, Massachusetts Air National Guard. The 101st flew from Otis Air National Guard Base on Cape Cod. The unit flew its last patrol mission on 24 January 2008, and its aircraft were transferred to the 104th Fighter Wing (ANG) at Barnes Airport, Massachusetts. (Nicholas A. Veronico)

The AMARG operating property has been divided into 29 areas, which enable an efficient aircraft inventory management. Aircraft are parked together by type within specific areas, and two of the property's parking areas contain aircraft tooling for the B-1, the B-2, and the A-10.

One of the eastern-most parking areas is used for Aircraft Battle Damage Repair (ABDR) and explosives testing. A number of commercial aircraft from the C-137 fleet were moved to this area to test the explosive containment properties of newly developed aircraft cargo containers. The containers were loaded into the bellies of the jetliners and suitcases laden with explosives were detonated. The resulting damage to the cargo container and the aircraft was studied to determine what materials were best suited to protect the flying public from potential terrorist attacks.

Within each parking area, aircraft are positioned on rows, and each space is individually numbered. Thus, an aircraft's serial number can be matched to the AMARG inventory number, which can then be matched to an exact parking location. As new aircraft arrive, or older aircraft go through preservation maintenance, inventory numbers are impacted and parking locations change. In addition, when AMARG receives advance notice that aircraft fleets will soon be retired, such as the C-141 and C-5 fleets recently, they must reposition aircraft in storage to make room for the influx of new arrivals.

Parked along the storage rows are many unique and historic aircraft, each with a story to tell, most with a special meaning to their former air or ground crewmembers. Not every aircraft can be saved, no matter the purpose or intention, thus unique paint schemes, insignia, and nose art that catch the eye are recorded here.

Early 1970s view of the storage facility at Davis-Monthan AFB, then known as the Military Aircraft Storage and Disposition Center, or MASDC. Lockheed C-121 Constellations and EC-121 (airborne, early-warning variants of the Constellation commercial airliner) were being phased out of service in favor of jet-powered aircraft. The cargo-carrying C-121s were replaced by another Lockheed aircraft, the C-141 Starlifter, while the EC-121s were replaced by Boeing E-3A Sentry Airborne Warning and Control System, or AWACS, aircraft. **(AMARG)**

As more and more C-141 Starlifters and KC-135 tankers came online in the late 1960s and early 1970s, piston-powered transports and tankers, such as the C-97 and KC-97, were removed from service. Although the C-97's Pratt & Whitney R-4360 engines were also being flown on the Douglas C-124, the majority of the -97's parts were excess to the military's needs. Here a field of C/KC-97s have had their engines and landing gear removed and are awaiting their fate with the scrap man. (AMARG)

Ground view showing the right-hand sides of four Douglas C-54 aircraft sitting on the ground or on blocks minus engines and landing gear with doors and hatches missing. Note the Blue Angels former support aircraft (C-54Q BuNo. 56508), which was retired in March 1968 and sold for scrap in December 1974. (Emil Strasser via Gerry Liang)

The R-4360 piston-powered C-124 Globemaster II fleet was retired en masse between 1972 and 1974. The majority were sold as lots to scrappers and was gone by the end of 1976. (Emil Strasser via Gerry Liang)

Boeing-Wichita-built B-29A 44-70016 was the last Superfortress at AMARG. The aircraft was saved to form the nucleus of what is now the Pima Air & Space Museum, across the road from AMARG, which opened on 8 May 1976. This aircraft flew 31 combat missions from Guam during World War II with the 20th Air Force, 330th Bomb Group's 458th Bomb Squadron as Sentimental Journey/Quaker City. The bomber later served with the 4713th Radar Evaluation and Electronic Countermeasures Flight at Griffiss AFB, New York, wearing the cartoon nose art of Dopey. (Brian R. Baker)

The second McDonnell Douglas F-15A to arrive at AMARG, serial number 71-0282, was delivered on 16 December 1977. This Eagle was the third F-15A prototype and was used primarily for avionics tests. It first flew on 4 November 1972, and was equipped with APG-63 radar. After two years in storage, the aircraft was returned to service with the 2955th Combat Logistics Support Squadron at Robins AFB, Georgia. (Brian R. Baker)

Aerial view of 62 General Dynamics F-16s parked in rows. Although the type is still a major component of the U.S. Air Force inventory, more than 400 Fighting Falcons are currently in storage at AMARG. (Nicholas A. Veronico)

Line of F-15s that have all had their search radars removed with 74-0106 (second from left) and 74-0123 (third from left), both having arrived from the 325th Fighter Wing, Tyndall AFB, Florida. (Nicholas A. Veronico)

Ex-199th Fighter Squadron (Hawaii ANG) F-15A 74-0135 arrived with a number of its squadron mates on 22 April 1992. The 199th is scheduled to transition to the F-22A Raptor beginning in late 2010. (Nicholas A. Veronico)

Former Air National Guard F-16s from Arizona, Illinois, Minnesota, North Dakota, and Texas sit with former 412th Test Wing, Edwards AFB, white-and-orange F-16B 80-0635. Most of these aircraft will most likely become full-scale aerial target drones in the coming years. (Ron Strong)

Davis-Monthan's storage inventory began with B-29s and C-47s. The majority of the B-29s were gone by 1961, but the C-47 Skytrain was another story. Affectionately known as the Gooney Bird, the aircraft saw service as a gunship in Vietnam, and an era ended on 2 March 1994, when the last Skytrain was sold. C-47D serial number 44-76642 was sold to Allied Aircraft Sales of Tucson, and then to Basler Turbo Conversions of Oshkosh, Wisconsin, and was trucked to its new home. This aircraft, delivered to the AAF on 30 March 1945, flew with the 12th Air Force in Italy, and was stateside with the Reconstruction Finance Corporation by 17 September 1945. Its last operational unit was the 380th Strategic Aerospace Wing and it was retired on 3 November 1969. The aircraft was photographed a few months before its departure on 20 July 1993. (Nicholas A. Veronico)

The 178th Fighter Squadron Happy Hooligans of the North Dakota Air National Guard flew the F-16A Air Defense Fighter (ADF) as part of the North American Air Defense Command (NORAD) protecting the northern border of the United States. The 178th was the last unit to fly the F-16 ADF. F-16A 81-0791 (closest to the camera) and F-16A 82-0950 both arrived at AMARG on 1 November 2006. (Ron Strong)

A trio of Fighting Falcons sits in storage prepared to provide parts to keep others flying. Former 412th Test Wing F-16 78-0007 arrived on 27 September 1994. Behind it can be seen ex-Alabama Air National Guard F-16A 80-0512 and F-16A 79-0341 from the 465th Fighter Squadron, Air Force Reserve. (Nicholas A. Veronico)

F-16A 79-0405 from the 106th Fighter Squadron, Alabama Air National Guard, is parked in front of F-16A 80-0475 from the 465th Fighter Squadron, Air Force Reserve based at Tinker AFB, Oklahoma. F-16A 79-0405 arrived for storage on 13 August 1993, and 80-0475 flew to AMARG on 22 March 1994. (Nicholas A. Veronico)

Just a portion of the more than 400 McDonnell Douglas F-4 Phantoms, and 37 Grumman F-14 Tomcats are visible. Most of the Tomcats have been shredded to prevent surplus parts from falling into the hands of foreign operators. (Nicholas A. Veronico)

Having last served with VF-32 Swordsmen onboard USS Harry S. Truman (CVN-75), F-14B, BuNo. 162691, was retired to AMARG on 21 September 2005. NAS Oceana, Virginia-based VF-32 received its first Tomcats in July 1974. Tomcat 162691 is seen wearing a retro scheme for the type's phase-out from VF-32 as the squadron transitioned into the new Boeing F/A-18F Super Hornet and was redesignated VFA-32. (Ron Strong)

F-14A 161866 last served with VF-154 Black Knights aboard USS Kitty Hawk (CV-63). During Operation Iraqi Freedom, VF-154 Tomcats flew as close air support and forward air controller aircraft. VF-154 flew the F-14 for 20 years before the type was phased out in favor of the new Super Hornet. This aircraft was retired on 23 October 2004. (Ron Strong)

VF-213 Black Lions F-14D 164602 wears a special paint scheme for the squadron's last cruise in 2006 before retiring the Tomcat. VF-213 was based aboard USS Theodore Roosevelt (CVN-71) and arrived at AMARG on 28 March 2006. (Ron Strong)

TA-4J BuNo. 154656 flew as a training aircraft with Training Wing Three (TW-3) from NAS Chase Field, Beeville, Texas. For carrier qualifications, TW-3 aircraft operated aboard USS Lexington (AVT-16). Coincidentally, the ship, training wing, and aircraft were all declared surplus within months of each other: BuNo. 154656 arrived at AMARG on 18 September 1991, the Lexington was decommissioned on 15 June 1992, to become a museum at Corpus Christi, Texas, and TW-3 was disestablished in October 1992. (Nicholas A. Veronico)

F-14B 162699 served with Air Test and Evaluation Squadron Nine (VX-9) at Naval Air Weapons Station China Lake, California. The aircraft arrived at AMARG on 23 June 2004. Ejection seats and other avionics have been removed and the canopy sits on the desert next to the jet. (Ron Strong)

F-14D 164345 was one of the last Tomcats to serve with VF-31, the Navy's last operational Tomcat squadron. VF-31 Tomcatters served aboard USS Theodore Roosevelt (CVN-71) as part of the Atlantic Fleet. BuNo. 164645's tail markings include the 2005 Golden Anchor award and Arleigh Burke Fleet Trophy. This aircraft arrived at AMARG on 15 September 2006. (Ron Strong)

Shortly after the type was phased out, there were F-14s lined up at AMARG as far as the eye could see. (Nicholas A. Veronico)

A-4s and TA-4s, with two VMA-214 A-4Ms visible. BuNo. 160026 arrived at AMARG on 26 May 1989, and at press time 160022 was still in the AMARG inventory while 160026 had been scrapped by HVF West. (Nicholas A. Veronico)

TA-4J BuNo. 152850 leads a row of training command TA-4s. Today, more than 150 Skyhawks are parked in rows at AMARG. Having been manufactured from 1954 through 1979, nearly 3,000 A-4s were built, with more than 500 being the two-seat TA-4 version seen here. The TA-4 also flew with the air forces and navies of six different allied nations. (Nicholas A. Veronico)

TA-4J 154632 wears the aggressor paint scheme of VF-126 Bandits based at NAS Miramar, California. VF-126 served as the Pacific Fleet Adversary Squadron providing air combat maneuvering training and ground schools for fleet pilots. BuNo. 154632 arrived at AMARG in March 1994, and VF-126 was disestablished that same year. (Nicholas A. Veronico)

TA-4J Skyhawk BuNo. 153461 last flew with VF-45 Blackbirds, an aggressor training squadron, as Lt. Patrick "Voodoo" Voors' Red 04. BuNo. 153461 arrived at AMARG on 13 July 1994. VF-45 was disestablished in March 1996. (Nicholas A. Veronico)

A-4M BuNo. 159492 of VMA-214 arrived on 1 June 1989, and was scrapped by HVF West in Tucson on 16 September 2004. TA-4J BuNo. 154614 CTW-1 arrived for storage on 23 May 1996, and was transferred to the U.S. Army as a parts aircraft to support other flying aircraft. (Nicholas A. Veronico)

The U.S. Navy parked most of its S-3 fleet in 2006. BuNo. 160121 from Sea Control Squadron Three Three (VS-33), the "World Famous and Internationally Traveled Screwbirds," arrived on 27 June of that year. The few remaining S-3 Vikings were retired from fleet service in January 2009. (Ron Strong)

Former VF-126 A-4F BuNo. 155018 wears a blue aggressor paint scheme. The aircraft arrived at AMARG on 28 March 1994, and is still in storage. (Nicholas A. Veronico)

Heavily picked over S-3As BuNo. 160593, last with VS-41, and ex-USS Ranger *S-3A 160574 of VS-38, the* Fighting Red Griffins, *were retired within days of each other. The Vikings arrived at AMARG on 30 October and 7 November 1991, respectively.* (Nicholas A. Veronico)

The Shamrocks of VS-41 received its first S-3 on 20 February 1974, and has logged more than 347,000 flight hours, made more than 48,000 carrier landings, and trained more than 35,000 people in the Viking. VS-41 S-3 BuNo. 159756 arrived at AMARG on 8 August 2006. The Navy is replacing the S-3 by having the F/A-18E/F Super Hornet, P-3, and SH-60 take up parts of the Viking's anti-submarine and aerial-refueling missions. (Ron Strong)

S-3B 160605 from VS-41 wears a black-and-yellow badge behind and below the pilot's canopy commemorating Torpedo Bomber Squadron 29/1960-2004. This aircraft arrived for storage on 1 August 2006. Although the official name of the Lockheed S-3 is the Viking, flight deck personnel aboard aircraft carriers affectionately named it "The Hoover," because the jet sounded like a big vacuum cleaner. (Ron Strong)

More than 400 F-4s and 66 F-14s are seen parked in this 1996 aerial view. Many of the F-4s have gone on to serve as aerial target drones while more than 400 remain in storage to this day. (Nicholas A. Veronico)

Among the F-4 Phantoms can be seen ex-Happy Hooligans (North Dakota ANG) F-4D 64-0979, which arrived at AMARG on 1 February 1990, ex-Oregon ANG F-4C 64-0711 that arrived on 23 October 1989, another ex-Happy Hooligans F-4D 64-0959 (4 January 1990), and ex-Michigan ANG F-4D 65-0590. Surprisingly, all four of these aircraft were present at AMARG in 2009. (Nicholas A. Veronico)

Row of F-4s led by ex-USS Coral Sea (CVA-43) Phantom (F-4N) BuNo. 152981 wearing the colors and "NK" tail code of VF-154 Black Knights. Originally built as an F-4B, this aircraft made its first flight on 3 February, 1966 and was retired to AMARG on 19 October 1983. (Armand H. Veronico)

When viewing the aircraft from the air, aircraft parking rows show the amount of room required to tow aircraft to and from the flight line. (Nicholas A. Veronico)

F-4B BuNo. 152208 made its first flight on 3 November 1964. Subsequently modified to F-4N configuration, the Phantom last served with Marine Attack Squadron Three One Four (VMFA-314). The aircraft was retired on 12 March 1982. On 10 November 2004, BuNo. 152208 was sold to HVF West and subsequently scrapped. (Nicholas A. Veronico)

The iconic all-black Phantom with Playboy bunny logo on the tail belongs to Air Test and Evaluation Squadron Four (VX-4) based at NAS Point Mugu, California. This F-4S BuNo. 155539, flew from Point Mugu to AMARG on 2 May 1986, where it awaits its fate. Its markings were inspired by the Douglas DC-9 executive jet once owned by Playboy Enterprises, Inc. (Ron Strong)

Two ex-Edwards AFB 6512th Test Squadron, 6510th Test Wing NF-4Es, 66-0291 and 66-0377, arrived at AMARG on 21 March and 15 April 1991, respectively. Both aircraft had flown with the U.S. Air Force Thunderbirds demonstration squadron before the team phased out the Phantom in favor of the T-38 and then the F-16 Fighting Falcon. (Ron Strong)

Having last served with VF-154, the Black Knights, onboard USS Coral Sea (CVA-43), F-4N BuNo. 153047 was retired on 19 October 1983. Here it sits as the dramatic dark clouds of a winter storm approach while a B-52G rests in the background. (Nicholas A. Veronico)

Standing out from the rest, a single McDonnell F-4 Phantom with spraylat sits among a row of bagged Navy F-4s. The Phantom was a multi-role tactical aircraft that flew for more than four decades with the air forces of twelve different countries. (Nicholas A. Veronico)

F-4N BuNo. 153027 wears the colors of VF-154's air group commander. This aircraft first flew on 19 July 1966, and was retired on 17 November 1983. The aircraft was scrapped on 10 November 2004, by HVF West in Tucson. (Nicholas A. Veronico)

While most of the Convair F-102 fleet was converted to supersonic drones, those that escaped the aerial target program spent nearly 30 years in storage before the last of the Delta Daggers were sold to scrappers in 1999. This F-102A escaped the scrapper's torch and was moved to the McChord AFB, Washington. TF-102A serial number 56-2350 (behind) was not so fortunate and was scrapped in 2000. (Nicholas A. Veronico)

In the middle of nearly 400 F-4 Phantoms sits F-4D 66-8705, which has been stored in a plastic bag rather than being preserved with spraylat. The bags can be used for up to eight years, which is equivalent to two spraylat coatings. F-4D 66-8705 first flew on 31 July 1967, and served until its retirement on 11 July 1989. The aircraft last served with the 170th Tactical Fighter Squadron of the Illinois Air National Guard and was scrapped 14 June 1999. (Nicholas A. Veronico)

The introduction of the B-47, B-52, and fast jet fighters signaled the need for a jet-powered aerial-refueling platform. This came in the form of the KC-135. As greater numbers of KC-135s came on line, the piston-powered KC-97 was quickly phased out of frontline service. KC-97 serial number 52-2617 was one of 592 G-models built. It sits minus its landing gear, props, cowls, radar, and engine cylinders just days from being recycled into aluminum ingots. (Brian R. Baker)

Lineup of Air Force F-4s, most having last served with the Happy Hooligans from the North Dakota Air National Guard. (Nicholas A. Veronico)

Row of Phantoms with reconnaissance-configured RF-4Cs 65-0896 and 68-0585 clearly visible. Both aircraft arrived at AMARC in March 1991 and were still present in 2009. (Nicholas A. Veronico)

Configured for the suppression of enemy air defenses, Wild Weasel Republic F-105G Thunderchief 63-8266 is seen shortly after its arrival on 1 July 1980. This aircraft last operated with the 35th Tactical Fighter Wing at George AFB, California. Ten years after its arrival, on 14 November 1990, the large fighter was sent to the Mid-America Air Museum in Liberal, Kansas, for display. The large radar dish above the F-105 is actually on a Grumman E-2C Hawkeye parked behind. (Brian R. Baker)

F-111E 68-0048 wearing the 428th Fighter Squadron's pirate insignia and the name Buccaneers. (Nicholas A. Veronico)

F-111D 68-0176 last flew with the 523rd Fighter Squadron, 27th Fighter Wing, Cannon AFB, New Mexico, and arrived for storage on 13 November 1992. At that time the F-111D and G models were replaced by improved F-111E and F models. (Nicholas A. Veronico)

Interesting photograph showing squadrons of General Dynamics F-111 Aardvarks lined up in the desert. Some of these aircraft can be seen with wings extended in this May 1996 aerial view of AMARG. (Nicholas A. Veronico)

F-111E 68-0049 served with the 77th Fighter Squadron, 20th Fighter Wing "Gamblers" at Upper Heyford, UK, and arrived for storage on 13 October 1993. This aircraft wears special nose art "77th Gambler's Last Deal"—four sevens and an ace—to commemorate the type's phase out and the unit's reactivation at Shaw AFB, South Carolina, in January 1994. (Nicholas A. Veronico)

Two of the last Republic F-105 Thunderchiefs await a new assignment. F-105D 60-5385 last served with the 149th Tactical Fighter Squadron, Virginia ANG, and arrived at AMARG on 12 June 1981. This aircraft was transferred to the Texas Aviation Historical Society in Dumas, Texas, on 21 July 2002. F-105D 59-1759's last operator was the 121st Tactical Fighter Squadron of the Washington, D.C., ANG. Having arrived at AMARG on 10 July 1981, 59-1759 was transferred to the Yanks Air Museum, Chino, California, on 31 July 2002, after more than 20 years in storage. (Nicholas A. Veronico)

Lineup of Northrop T-38A Talons with 62-3732 (last serving with the 14th Fighter Training Wing), 63-8202 (47th Fighter Training Wing), and 62-3671 (14th Fighter Training Wing) visible behind. These supersonic trainers were retired in 1992 and 1993, and remain at AMARG providing parts to other flying aircraft. (Nicholas A. Veronico)

Northrop AT-38B Talon serial number 62-3614 wears blue camouflage and carries the HM tail code of 479th Tactical Training Wing at Holloman AFB, New Mexico. Pilots flying the AT-38B with the 479th used the supersonic fighter for lead-in training prior to transitioning to the F-15 Eagle. (Nicholas A. Veronico)

Aerial view of the mainstay of attack aircraft from the 1960s to the 1990s: Grumman A-6 Intruders (foreground) and LTV A-7s (above and to the left). (Nicholas A. Veronico)

FB-111A 68-0292 sits in the reclamation area. This aircraft yielded many parts to keep other FB-111s flying. (Nicholas A. Veronico)

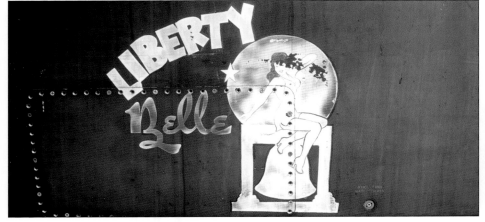

FB-111A 68-0292 from the 380th Bomb Wing at Plattsburgh AFB, New York, wears the nose art of Liberty Belle. This aircraft entered storage on 5 June 1991 and, after being picked clean of useable parts, was scrapped on 28 February 2001. The supersonic General Dynamics F-111 was the Air Force's first variable-geometry, or "swing-wing," aircraft. (Nicholas A. Veronico)

F-111G 68-0273 arrived at AMARG on 22 May 1991, from the 428th Tactical Fighter Training Squadron, 27th Tactical Fighter Wing. G-models serving with the 428th were FB-111As from the Strategic Air Command that had their nuclear weapons capacity removed and were fitted with a digital avionics suite. This aircraft was scrapped by 1 April 1997. (Nicholas A. Veronico)

McDonnell RF-101C 56-0115 was one of the last reconnaissance-configured Voodoos to survive at AMARG. This aircraft last served with the 153rd Tactical Reconnaissance Squadron, Mississippi Air National Guard, and arrived on 12 January 1979. It was sent to the scrapper on 12 August 1999. (Nicholas A. Veronico)

Air Force Ling-Temco-Vought (LTV) A-7D 70-1031 wears the tail code PR of the 198th Fighter Squadron, Puerto Rico Air National Guard. Today there are fewer than 90 A-7s in storage. (Nicholas A. Veronico)

A-6Es BuNos. 151802 (foreground) and 164383 both wear NK tail codes of VA-196 serving aboard USS Carl Vinson (CVN-70). BuNo. 151802 at one time served with VX-5 at Naval Air Weapons Station (NAWS) China Lake, California. (Nicholas A. Veronico)

A row of Navy A-7s led by BuNo. 154520, which last served with VA-204 River Rattlers, a Naval Reserve squadron located at NAS New Orleans, Louisiana. In April 1991, VA-204 was redesignated Strike Fighter Squadron Two Zero Four (VFA-204) and transitioned from the A-7 Corsair II to the F/A-18 Hornet. (Nicholas A. Veronico)

Single- and two-seat LTV A-7 Corsairs parked side by side. On the left is former Arizona Air National Guard A-7K 79-0466 and on the right is ex-U.S. Navy A-7E BuNo. 158831. The A-7K arrived on 27 December 1990 and, although still in storage, was transferred to the U.S. Navy on 14 June 2001. A-7E 158831 is also currently in storage. (Ron Strong)

Grumman EA-6 Prowler electronic warfare aircraft sit among A-6 Intruders in storage. The A-6 has been phased out of service and the EA-6 is currently being replaced by the F/A-18G Growler. Two EA-6As are identifiable with BuNo. 156987 (closest to the camera) and 156983 (to the rear). Both aircraft arrived for storage on 6 July 1993, having last flown with Tactical Electronics Warfare Squadron Three Three (VAQ-33), Night Hawks, based at NAS Quonset Point, Rhode Island. (Ron Strong)

Grumman A-6E Intruder BuNo. 159579 wears the colors of the Commander Air Group, or CAG-bird, of Carrier Air Wing 14 (CAW-14) based aboard the nuclear-powered USS Carl Vinson (CVN-70). This attack aircraft was assigned to Medium Attack Squadron (VA-196) tail code NK. Note the low-visibility, or "lo-vis" national insignia and NAVY title still visible on the rear fuselage, an ironic combination when seen together with the aircraft's colorful vertical stabilizer. (Nicholas A. Veronico)

Convair F-106B 59-0164 has given up its main gear to keep another Delta Dart in the air. This aircraft was the second-to-last F-106B built. The two-seat interceptor was delivered to the 329th Fighter Interceptor Squadron at George AFB, California, in January 1961. In August 1962, the aircraft went south to the 4756th Air Defense Group at Tyndall AFB, Florida, where it flew until retirement on 4 April 1984. Ten years later, the aircraft's nose section went to the Southern Utah Air Museum as an educational tool. (Nicholas A. Veronico)

Convair F-106s in storage prior to being returned to flight status for the full-scale aerial target program. During the early 1990s, AMARG returned 199 F-106s for the drone program. (Armand H. Veronico)

Marine Attack Training Squadron Two Zero Three (VMAT-203) Hawks of Marine Corps Air Station (MCAS) Cherry Point, North Carolina, used two-seat TAV-8A Harriers to train both air and ground crews on the operations of the Vertical Takeoff and Landing (VTOL) attack fighter. BuNo. 159378 is one of eight TAV-8As built by Hawker Siddeley Aviation Ltd., of Surrey, England, between 1975 and 1976. All of the Hawker Siddeley-built trainers were phased out of service in October and November 1987 after new McDonnell Douglas-built TAV-8B Harrier IIs came on line beginning in 1986. (Nicholas A. Veronico)

AV-8C Harrier BuNo. 158973 from Marine Attack Squadron Five Four Two (VMA-542) Tigers surrounded by North American T-2s. This aircraft missed VMA-542's participation in Operation Desert Storm having been sent to storage in April 1986. On 16 November 2004, 158973 departed AMARG to become a range target at Fort Sill, Oklahoma. (Nicholas A. Veronico)

Convair F-106A Delta Dart (59-0012) was delivered in December 1959 and spent its entire operational career at Minot AFB, North Dakota. On 6 May 1960, the Delta Dart was assigned to the 5th Fighter Interceptor Squadron, 32nd Fighter Group. Over the years the Fighter Group's name changed to Fighter Wing and the Air Defense Command evolved into the Tactical Air Command, but 59-0012 remained at Minot. On 3 April 1985, 59-0012 was phased out of the active inventory and sent to storage. In November 2003 the aircraft was trucked to the Barry M. Goldwater Bombing Range, Gila Bend, Arizona, to become a target. Parts of 59-0012 were salvaged to restore the McChord Air Museum's F-106, serial number 56-0459. (Nicholas A. Veronico)

Within a row of Sikorsky H-53s of various models, individual aircraft can be easily identified. Closest to the camera wearing inventory number AAHC0026 is TH-53A Super Jolly Green Giant 66-4472, which arrived for storage on 27 July 2001. Inventory number AAHC0028 (TH-53A 67-0046) arrived the same day, and the third helicopter in the row, AAHC0046, is MH-53M Sea Dragon 69-5784, which entered storage on 14 November 2007. The largest single-rotor cabin helicopter used by the U.S. military, the amphibious H-53 series first flew in 1969 and continued for nearly four decades. (Ron Strong)

Sikorsky CH-53D Sea Stallion BuNo. 157930 last served with Marine Helicopter Squadron One (HMX-1), the Nighthawks. HMX-1 transports the President of the United States, vice president, and other members of the government. Should the president be aboard one of its helicopters, that HMX-1 rotorcraft would be designated "Marine One." Sea Stallion 157930 was stored on 25 November 1996, and was sold on 7 October 2002, to provide parts for Heavy Lift Helicopters' two commercially operated CH-53Ds. After parts reclamation, the carcasses were returned to AMARG. (Ron Strong)

NASA used this F-106A, serial number 59-0130, for its Eclipse Project. Based at the Dryden Flight Research Center at Edwards AFB, California, and working with the U.S. Air Force and a private company, Kelly Space and Technology Inc., the Eclipse Project demonstrated the towed launch vehicle concept using a Lockheed C-141A Starlifter (61-2775) to tow the F-106 aloft. This combination was used to determine if a space vehicle could be towed to 40,000 feet and subsequently launched into orbit. Tow launching theoretically enables a greater payload versus a vertical, rocket-boosted launch. The Eclipse Project validated the potential of towing a delta-wing vehicle to altitude for use as a launch platform. (Nicholas A. Veronico)

F-106 59-0043 was used to protect America's northern borders from March 1960 to 23 January 1973, flying from Loring AFB, Maine, and Dover AFB, Delaware. On 24 January 1973, 59-0043 was transferred to the 119th Fighter Interceptor Squadron, 177th Fighter Interceptor Group, Jersey Devils, based at Atlantic City, New Jersey. When the New Jersey ANG retired the type, 59-0043 was specially marked to commemorate the event. Spirit of Atlantic City also lists the units that flew the Delta Dart on the right side of the nose. Col. Joe Rogers used F-106 56-0467 to set a world speed record of 1525.95 mph on 15 December 1959, which is commemorated on the left rear of the Spirit of Atlantic City. Subsequent to its retirement in 1988, 59-0043 went to the F-106 drone program, hence the high-visibility drone markings. The Delta Dart was returned to storage in March 1998. (Nicholas A. Veronico)

Helicopter parking in area 21 with Bell TH-57 Sea Rangers, UH-1 Iroquois, and AH-1 Cobras. (Ron Strong)

Four Bell AH-1Js formerly with Marine Attack Helicopter Squadron Seven Seven Three (HMA-773) Red Dogs, a Marine Reserve squadron operating from NAS Atlanta, Georgia. HMA-773 was activated for the Gulf War, and the helicopters here probably have combat history flying mine-sweeping escort and other missions from USS New Orleans and USS Tripoli. The AH-1Js (from left to right: BuNos. 159225, 157798, 157760, and 157768) were traded for AH-1W Super Cobras in fall 1992. (Ron Strong)

Sikorsky SH-3G Sea King, BuNo. 149723, was last operated by NASA at the space agency's Ames Research Center in Mountain View, California. NASA 735 arrived at AMARG on 27 July 1993, and is currently in storage in late 2009. During the 1960s, Sea Kings served as the Navy's primary carrier-based helicopter flying patrol, supply, and rescue missions that included the recovery of Gemini and Apollo astronauts returning from space. (Nicholas A. Veronico)

Intended for the Imperial Iranian Army, AH-1J 3-4412 was under construction during the height of the Iran hostage crisis, which lasted 444 days from 4 November 1979 to 20 January 1981. When the Shah of Iran was deposed the aircraft's delivery was canceled; it was delivered to AMARG on 5 June 1980, and the helicopter has spent its entire life in the Arizona desert. (Ron Strong)

Palletized Northrop T-38 Talon 63-8148 arrived from the San Antonio Air Logistics Center by truck on 3 April 1996. Six years later it had given up enough parts to the flying fleet that it was scrapped. (Nicholas A. Veronico)

KC-130F BuNo. 150690 arrived for storage on 2 February 2006, from Marine Aerial Refueler Transport Squadron One Five Two (VMGR-152), known as the Sumos. This squadron operates out of MCAS Futenma, Okinawa, Japan, and flies with the QD tail code. Before joining the Sumos, 150690 was the first C-130 to fly with the Blue Angels and was the aircraft that earned the nickname "Fat Albert." Now, all Marine C-130s that support the Navy's aerial demonstration squadron are called Fat Albert, but this is the one that started the tradition. (Ron Strong)

Ski-equipped Lockheed LC-130F BuNo. 148321 last served with Antarctic Development Squadron Six (VXE-6) supporting polar research on behalf of the National Science Foundation. The flights, known as Operation Deep Freeze, took place every year from October through February, and the squadron spent the summers training at Naval Air Weapons Station Point Mugu, California. The squadron supported its last Operation Deep Freeze during the winter of 1998/1999, and the aircraft arrived for storage on 29 March 1999. (Nicholas A. Veronico)

Lockheed AC-130A gunship, christened Night Stalker, wears nose art with five camels and one crab. This gunship saw extensive service in Vietnam flying support missions from Ubon Royal Thai Air Force Base, Thailand. It last saw service with the 711th Special Operations Squadron, 919th Special Operations Group, out of Duke Field, Florida. With that unit it participated in Operation Just Cause in Panama and Operation Desert Storm. Night Stalker was retired to AMARG on 15 November 1994. (Nicholas A. Veronico)

The career of AC-130A 55-0029, Midnight Express, mirrored that of Night Stalker. Midnight Express was also flown to storage on 15 November 1994. (Nicholas A. Veronico)

Assigned to the 89th Military Airlift Wing, the unit responsible for flying U.S. government officials, the VC-140B could be called upon to serve as Air Force One when necessary. Six VC-140Bs were built. VC-140B serial number 62-4199 sits minus its landing gear and wing panels in this May 1996 photo. It was delivered to storage on 10 February 1984 and sold for scrap on 18 April 2001. (Nicholas A. Veronico)

Lockheed's C-140 JetStar had a crew of two and could seat ten passengers in the main cabin. This business-class jet, C-140B 62-4200, served as a mission support aircraft and was one of five that were fitted with a convertible interior so they could carry passengers or, by removing the interior seating, they could carry high-priority cargo. C-140B 62-4200 last served with the 58th Military Airlift Squadron and was stored on 18 June 1987; it was sold for scrap on 21 March 1995. (Nicholas A. Veronico)

The aircraft fitted with the bulbous nose is Boeing EC-135E 61-0326, an Advanced Range Instrument Aircraft, or ARIA. These aircraft were used to collect trajectory information on space-craft and missiles. The bulbous nose is a 10-foot radome that protects a 7-foot-diameter dish antenna. NASA first developed ARIA aircraft for use in the Apollo program. Eight Air Force aircraft were modified for the program in 1975, which were supplemented with eight ex-American Airlines 707s (redesignated EC-18Bs) in 1982. This aircraft was last flown with the 412th Test Wing at Edwards AFB, California, and was retired on 1 June 1998. (Nicholas A. Veronico)

Air Force Convair VT-29Ds, the first in line from the Montana Air National Guard and wearing Big Sky Country markings, were military versions of the Convair 340 airliner. These aircraft were often used to transport command staffs or military attachés and their staffs. (Nicholas A. Veronico)

A row of Lockheed T-33 Shooting Stars, the Air Force's long-serving jet trainer, with ex-318th Fighter Interceptor Squadron T-33A 58-0506 and ex-95th Fighter Interceptor Training Squadron T-33A 58-0500 in view. (Nicholas A. Veronico)

The Martin B-57 was the American license-built version of the British English Electric Canberra bomber. The aerial view (top photo) shows the wing planform of the WB-57 with standard B-57s to the right (bottom row). Also seen in the aerial view are F-15s and T-2s (middle row), and F-111s, more T-2s, T-37s, OV-1s, and C-130s (top row) in various states of repair. The engine was mounted right through the wing as seen on WB-57F 63-13302 (above left and right). The WB-57F was a high-altitude reconnaissance conversion of the B-57B fitted with an enlarged 122-foot wing, of which 17 were so modified. (Nicholas A. Veronico)

Two survivors of the F-100 full-scale aerial target program are F-100Fs 56-3837 and 56-3832. The National Museum of the U.S. Air Force acquired 56-3837 on 18 June 2002, and the Evergreen Aviation Museum in McMinnville, Oregon, took delivery of 56-3832 in May 2004. Only one Super Sabre remains and that aircraft is on AMARG's Celebrity Row. (Nicholas A. Veronico)

T-33A serial number 52-9848 arrived at AMARG on 19 September 1986, and is also an ex-95th Fighter Interceptor Training Squadron aircraft from Tyndall AFB, Florida. Derived from the famed Lockheed P-80 Shooting Star, the T-33 produced more Air Force jet pilots than any previous training aircraft. T-33s flew with the USAF as squadron hacks well into the 1980s. (Nicholas A. Veronico)

Sitting on Celebrity Row is AMARG's last Lockheed T-1 SeaStar (previously known as the T2V). The aircraft featured a raised rear canopy and a more powerful J33-A-24 engine of 6,100 pounds static thrust than its T-33/TV-2 predecessors. One prototype and 150 production T-1s were built. The Navy replaced the T-1 with the North American T-2 Buckeye. (Ron Strong)

Republic F-84F Thunderstreak serial number 52-6563 lives on today having donated major assemblies to the aircraft now displayed at the Pima Air & Space Museum, south of AMARG. (Nicholas A. Veronico)

Air Force serial number 53-7600 was one of 715 Republic RF-84F Thunderflash high-speed aerial reconnaissance aircraft built at the height of the Cold War. After frontline service, the RF-84F equipped a number of Air National Guard squadrons, including the 106th Tactical Reconnaissance Squadron, Alabama ANG. Serial number 53-7600 was delivered to the desert storage facility on 12 March 1971. When it could not find a museum willing to take on the restoration, the aircraft was scrapped on 23 June 1999. (Nicholas A. Veronico)

Ex-Idaho Air National Guard TF-102 serial number 56-2350 was the last two-seat Delta Dagger in the AMARG inventory. It arrived on 23 October 1975, and was scrapped on 22 June 1999. TF-102 initially wore the all-gray color scheme of the USAF Air Defense Command. (Nicholas A. Veronico)

Leading a row of North American Rockwell T-2C Buckeyes are BuNos. 156727 and 158331. The Buckeye was the standard U.S. Navy intermediate jet trainer from 1959 to 2008. Both of these aircraft last flew with Training Wing Two (TW-2), the Professionals, based at NAS Kingville, Texas. (Nicholas A. Veronico)

An impressive row of Navy Training Command T-2C Buckeyes as seen from the rear. The Buckeye served as the stalwart jet trainer for every naval aviator who ever flew jet fighters from aircraft carriers, including their first jet solo and first carrier landings. (Nicholas A. Veronico)

The side profile of T-2C BuNo. 156727 shows the amount of the aircraft surface covered with spraylat preservative. With proper maintenance of the preservative materials, this aircraft can be stored for more than 40 years. (Nicholas A. Veronico)

Lockheed SP-2H Neptune BuNo. 147963 arrived for storage from VP-69, Totems, from NAS Whidbey Island, Washington, on 15 August 1975. In May 1980 the aircraft was transferred to U.S. Air Force control with two other SP-2Hs. The other two, BuNos. 144681 and 150282, were sold to a civilian company for conversion to air tankers. BuNo. 147963 was still in storage in September 2008. (Nicholas A. Veronico)

Fleet Air Reconnaissance Squadron One (VQ-1) was the last operator of Douglas EA-3B Skywarrior. This aircraft, BuNo. 142671, arrived on 28 April 1989, as the type neared the end of its service life with the U.S. Navy, and was sent to be scrapped on 11 January 2005. The A-3 Skywarrior has the distinction of being the largest and heaviest operational carrier-based aircraft in the history of naval aviation. (Armand H. Veronico)

Douglas EA-3B Skywarrior BuNo. 146455 has been an AMARG resident since 9 September 1991. This aircraft last flew with Fleet Air Reconnaissance Squadron Two (VQ-2), the Batmen, based at Rota, Spain, one of the last active duty Skywarrior squadrons. Today only 15 Skywarriors are parked at AMARG. (Ron Strong)

Rows of Grumman S-2 Tracker anti-submarine warfare patrol bombers sit among AV-8 Harriers and Vought A-7 Corsair IIs in a Navy aircraft parking area. S-2s served as the backbone of the Navy's carrier-based anti-submarine patrol arm from the mid 1950s through the late 1960s. (Nicholas A. Veronico)

T-2C BuNo. 158904 ended its U.S. Navy career with Fighter Squadron Four Three (VF-43). The Buckeye was flown to storage on 21 September 1993, and on 26 May 2000, was sold to Greece through the Foreign Military Sales Program. (Nicholas A. Veronico)

U.S. Marine Corps North American CT-39E BuNo. 160056 flew to storage on 28 October 1993, where it sat for almost five years. On 3 June 1998, 160056 was recalled to duty, overhauled, and delivered to the Futenma Marine Corps Air Station, Japan, where it now serves the station flight transporting light cargo and personnel around Okinawa and other Japanese islands. (Nicholas A. Veronico)

The U.S. Naval Air Weapons Center at Lakehurst, New Jersey, operated a number of C-28As, the military version of the Cessna 404 Titan. Two C-28As from Lakehurst were sent to storage on 24 January 1996. They were subsequently transferred to the U.S. Border Patrol on 8 February 2001. This C-28A, BuNo. 163917, was registered N97BP for its new operator. (Nicholas A. Veronico)

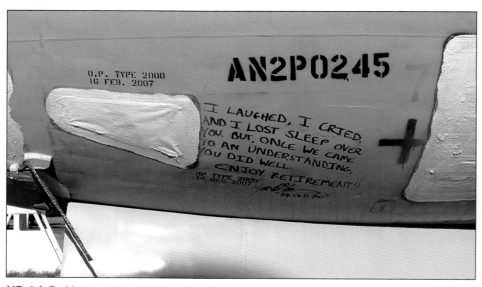

VP-3A BuNo. 149676 was delivered to the U.S. Navy on 6 October 1962, and served with a number of squadrons over the years, including VP-8 and VP-30. It also served as a weather reconnaissance aircraft (WP-3A) before being converted into a VIP transport. This aircraft was certainly a world traveler, and in the years prior to its retirement was spotted in Australia, Belgium, England, and Poland. Above the nose landing gear doors one of the Orion's former crewmembers summed up their affection for the aircraft by writing: "I laughed, I cried, and I lost sleep over you. But, once we came to an understanding, you did well. Enjoy retirement!!" (Ron Strong)

Here are rows of P-3s that may one day return to flight status, possibly with a foreign operator. Should there be no recall to duty, they will begin to yield parts to keep other aircraft flying. Notice that the landing gear wells are sealed to keep out moisture and unwanted guests. (Ron Strong)

Well-weathered S-2E BuNo. 149873, formerly of Navy Antisubmarine Warfare Squadron Eight Two (VS-82), received a new lease on life on 3 February 2000. The aircraft had been in storage for 26 years when the call to duty came from the California Department of Forestry and Fire Protection. The CDF, now known as CalFire, needed additional S-2 airframes that it planned to convert to turboprop power. BuNo. 149873 was removed from storage and converted to "Turbo Tracker" configuration by Marsh Aviation. Equipped with a 1,200-gallon retardant tank and registered N440DF, the aircraft now fights fires from any one of CalFire's 13 air attack bases. (Nicholas A. Veronico)

Lockheed's P-3 Orion began life as the Electra turboprop-powered commercial airliner, which first flew in 1957. The military's need for a long-range maritime patrol and anti-submarine warfare aircraft saw the U.S. Navy select the Electra design for its new patrol aircraft. The P-3 is 7 feet shorter than the commercial Electra, and includes numerous other structural modifications and mission-related hardware. In addition to the United States, 17 other nations fly the Orion. BuNo. 160286 (closest to the camera) was last operated by VP-26 and arrived on 7 December 2004. BuNo. 156518 (second in line) was flown by VP-30 before its retirement on 11 February 2004. (Ron Strong)

Aerial view of a row of 20 Lockheed P-3 Orions with a variety of C-130 Hercules transports in the distance. (Nicholas A. Veronico)

NAS Keflavik, Iceland's station aircraft, UP-3A
BuNo. 150495, wears the Valkyrie's head on its tail
and carries the Norse mythological name Valkyrja.
The base commander's name, Capt. Mark S.
Laughton, is painted under the pilot's side window.
(Ron Strong)

McDonnell Douglas built 21 C-9As at its Long Beach, California, factory between 1967 and 1972. Equipped for the aeromedical evacuation role, the Nightingale features a built-in stretcher ramp, and an 81-inch by 136-inch upward-swinging port-side cargo door. The C-9A is equivalent to the DC-9-32CF commercial jetliner. C-9A 68-8932 is named after the city of Fairview Heights, near Scott AFB, Illinois, where the aircraft was based. These C-9As show "UNITED STATES AIR FORCE," titles, but several received "UNITED STATES OF AMERICA" (see below) when they had to fly into countries that were politically sensitive to U.S. military presence. (Ron Strong)

U.S. Navy C-9B BuNo. 164605, City of San Diego, wears the tail code RX of Fleet Logistics Support Squadron Five Seven (VR-57), the Conquistadors. The RX tail code should not be lost on a squadron that flies aeromedical evacuations. In Spring 2005, VR-57 traded its C-9Bs in for Boeing C-40A Clippers. BuNo. 164605 was originally built as a DC-9-33 (manufacturer's serial number 47545) for the Spanish carrier Iberia and was delivered on 8 August 1972. In April 1990, McDonnell Douglas accepted the DC-9 as a trade-in against new jetliners and subsequently sold this aircraft to the U.S. Navy on 12 July 1990. (Ron Strong)

Air Force C-9As were called Nightingales; Navy C-9Bs were named Skymaster IIs. Nine of the 16 C-9A Nightingales are seen in this 2008 view. The majority of the C-9s were retired in August and September 2003. (Ron Strong)

C-9A 68-10958 was originally delivered to the Air Force on 30 September 1969, and was last flown by the 375th Air Wing. After 34 years of service, Swansea was retired to AMARG on 25 August 2003. (Ron Strong)

T-43A 71-1405 from the 12th Flying Training Wing (12th FTW) at Randolph AFB, Texas, used this aircraft for navigator training. The T-43, a military version of the Boeing 737, joined the 12th FTW in 1992. T-43A 71-1405 was placed in storage on 19 April 2005. (Ron Strong)

Parked among a gaggle of Douglas EA-3s and rows of Lockheed C-141s, Grumman C-2A Greyhound BuNo. 162151 last flew with Fleet Logistics Support Squadron Four Zero (VRC-40), the Rawhides. The unit provides carrier on-board delivery (COD) services to aircraft carriers in the Atlantic fleet. BuNo. 162151 arrived at AMARG on 10 August 2000. The C-2A utilized the same cockpit, wing, and engine as the E-2 Hawkeye, but had a larger fuselage, modified tail configuration, and aft-fuselage cargo ramp to facilitate carrier-based cargo loading operations. (Ron Strong)

The Grumman E-2 Hawkeye is a carrier-based airborne early-warning aircraft capable of observing 6 million cubic miles of airspace, from the surface to 50,000 feet, on each sweep of its radar. E-2C BuNo. 161783 was an integral part of Carrier Airborne Early Warning Squadron Seven Seven (VAW-77), the Night Wolves, which are unique among Hawkeye units. VAW-77 is based at Naval Air Station (Joint Reserve Base) New Orleans and serves to control and direct America's anti-drug smuggling forces in the Gulf of Mexico region. The squadron upgraded to the E-2C+ in 2005. (Ron Strong)

E-2C 163024 wears the colors of Carrier Airborne Early Warning Squadron One Two Six (VAW-126), the Seahawks. In December 2002, VAW-126 sailed aboard USS Harry S. Truman (CVN-75) to support forces in Operation Iraqi Freedom. The unit set a record of 100 sorties in 445 hours before returning to Norfolk in May 2003. BuNo. 163024 wears the nose art "Give 'Em Hell!" and 34 electronic mission marks from Operation Iraqi Freedom. This aircraft arrived at AMARG for storage on 11 July 2003, shortly after returning home. Its radome has been removed to provide parts for other aircraft flying with the fleet. (Ron Strong)

At one time, nearly 40 Martin-Marietta Titan II Intercontinental Ballistic Missiles (ICBM) were in storage at AMARG. Once a backbone deterrent weapon of the Cold War, the now-obsolete missiles will soon be scrapped. (Nicholas A. Veronico)

The first two of 17 Lockheed D-21s to arrive at AMARG are still in storage, even after many of their stablemates have gone on to be displayed at various aviation museums around the country. To augment the capabilities of the new Blackbird family of Mach 3 reconnaissance aircraft, Lockheed designed and developed the super-secret ramjet-powered D-21 drone. The D-21 was intended to be launched by a Blackbird, overfly denied territory, and then launch a camera package, which would be recovered by parachute. (Nicholas A. Veronico)

When operational, the Lockheed D-21 drone was top secret. They were then moved to Davis-Monthan for storage in 1976 and 1977 and became a favorite stop on the boneyard tour. They were quickly tagged as secret and taken off the tour until the early 1990s when the D-21's launch platform, the MD-11/A-12/SR-71 family of triple-sonic Blackbird aircraft, were phased out. Test launches of the D-21 were also accomplished from underwing pylons using the B-52H. (Nicholas A. Veronico)

Sitting minus its radome is E-2C BuNo. 161345, in the markings of the Naval Air Warfare Center—Aircraft Division. This aircraft was sent for storage on September 21, 1993. The aircraft's wings were folded for storage on the hangar or flight deck of an aircraft carrier. (Ron Strong)

Row of E-2Cs led by BuNo. 162802 from Carrier Airborne Early Warning Squadron Seven Eight (VAW-78), the Fighting Escargots. BuNo. 162802 was sent to storage on 18 October 2004, and VAW-78 was deactivated on 31 March 2005, after nearly 35 years of service. (Ron Strong)

U.S. Army Grumman OV-1D Mohawk serial number 67-18903 of the 641st Military Intelligence Battalion, Oregon Air National Guard, arrived on 11 December 1991, and is now a resident of Celebrity Row. The turboprop Mohawk was developed for the Army's Counter-Insurgency mission at the same time as Grumman's Gulfstream transport. (Ron Strong)

One of the last Cessna O-2A Skymasters in storage is 68-11167 from the U.S. Air Force's 25th Tactical Air Support Squadron. This aircraft was sent to storage on 14 July 1986, and was transferred to the U.S. Navy on 2 May 1994. The Skymaster is one of approximately 26 twin-engine Cessna O-2s in storage today. (Ron Strong)

Although looking a bit forlorn, there is one Teledyne-Ryan BQM-34 Firebee target drone in storage. Built as a BQM-34F, it has sat at AMARG since 17 May 1999. (Nicholas A. Veronico)

Coast Guard HU-25A Falcon is a medium-range surveillance aircraft based on the Dassault Falcon Jet business aircraft. The aircraft sensor package determines its model number, whether it is an HU-25A, -25B, or -25C. HU-25A serial number 2116 is one of 23 Falcons held in storage to provide spare aircraft or parts support as necessary. Cape Cod was 2116's last assignment. (Nicholas A. Veronico)

When parting-out large aircraft, sometimes subassemblies remain when the rest of the aircraft is gone. These B-52 tail turrets were last used on the G model, and were sent to the scrapper when the type was retired from active duty and there was no longer a need to support this type of gunnery system. (Nicholas A. Veronico)

SCRAPPING THE BIG FLEETS

The first Convair B-36 to arrive at Davis-Monthan begins the defueling process as ground crews work to drain the liquids from the bomber's engines. Light oil will be run through the fuel system and the engine to preserve the powerplants while the bombers await their final fate. (Frederick A. Johnsen Collection)

orty-three years after the Wright Brothers' history-making flight at Kill Devil Hills, North Carolina, America's first true intercontinental nuclear bomber was leaving the drawing board and would soon dominate the Cold War skies. The Consolidated B-36 Peacemaker was an aerial giant— six 3,800-horsepower, 4,360-cubic-inch piston engines driving 19-foot-diameter propellers supplemented by four 5,200-pound-thrust General Electric J47 turbojet engines hung under its 230-foot-wide wings. Known as the "Magnesium Overcast," the Peacemaker's fuselage was more than 162 feet long and could house a 10,000-pound bomb load to be carried more than 3,500 miles.

A little more than a dozen years later, the B-36 was rendered obsolete by new aviation technologies. The jet engine signaled the end of the Peacemaker when Boeing's new all-jet-powered B-52 Stratofortress became operational with the Strategic Air Command (SAC) in June 1956 and superseded the B-36. The first 53 B-36s to be retired started arriving at the Arizona Aircraft Storage Branch two months later. The B-36s were first stripped of their jet engines and propellers, and then their R-4360 piston engines were removed. After that process, it was a matter of reducing the fuselage to smaller pieces that would fit into the smelter. Along with the B-36s, early-model straight-wing Republic F-84 Thunderjets were unceremoniously stacked five airplanes high to await their turn in the smelter's furnace.

The B-36 fleet is framed by a quarter-mile-long fence of three-blade propellers as the aircraft await the scrapper's torch. Additional Peacemakers can be seen in the upper left corner. **(AMARG)**

One last B-36 escaped the scrapper's torch and on 30 April 1959, B-36J serial number 52-2220 was flown from Davis-Monthan to the Air Force Museum at Wright-Patterson AFB, Ohio. On 25 July 1961, the last B-36 was cut apart, making the Peacemaker the first of the big fleets to meet its end at Davis-Monthan.

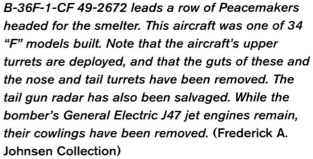

B-36F-1-CF 49-2672 leads a row of Peacemakers headed for the smelter. This aircraft was one of 34 "F" models built. Note that the aircraft's upper turrets are deployed, and that the guts of these and the nose and tail turrets have been removed. The tail gun radar has also been salvaged. While the bomber's General Electric J47 jet engines remain, their cowlings have been removed. (Frederick A. Johnsen Collection)

Late-1960s aerial view of the storage area with C-119s in the foreground, H-19s and H-21s (middle center), and Stratojets as far as the eye can see. (AMARG)

B-47E 53-2104 wears the Strategic Air Command "Milky Way" band on its nose section, awaiting the scrapper's torch in March 1979. (Harrison W. Rued)

B-47E 53-2039, also a Douglas-Tulsa-built example, is about to be towed to its parking place after being processed for storage in 1966. (Brian R. Baker)

Thirty-two RB-47Hs were built by Boeing at Wichita, Kansas. The number 27 aircraft off the production line was 53-4304, which is seen undergoing parts reclamation in March 1976. (Harrison W. Rued)

B-47s in the parts reclamation area, some with engines or radar removed, line the perimeter fence. America's first all-jet, swept-wing bomber fleet nears the end of its days. (Harrison W. Rued)

Douglas-Tulsa-built B-47E serial number 53-2135 represents its type on Celebrity Row in January 1976. More than 1,000 Stratojets were recycled at Davis-Monthan. **(Harrison W. Rued)**

One of the smelters at Davis-Monthan was busy devouring Stratojets in the mid 1970s. Here, a pair of B-47s are ready to be sliced by the crane's steel guillotine blade. **(Emil Strasser via Gerry Liang)**

Boeing-Wichita-built B-47E 53-2308 (at the end of the line) nears the scrapper's guillotine blade. This aircraft will soon become so many aluminum ingots. **(Harrison W. Rued)**

B-47Es 51-5257 and 51-2380 reduced to tail sections. Metallurgists are able to determine how clean each aircraft section's alloy will be once melted, thus similar aircraft sections are fed into the smelter in groups. **(Harrison W. Rued)**

Tails of 52-0485, 53-1903, 53-1888, 52-0486, 53-2161, 52-0294, and 53-1970 await their turn in the smelter. The cleaner the alloy, the more money the metal recycler will pay for aircraft scrap. **(Harrison W. Rued)**

Smelter belches flame as it awaits more Stratojet parts. Once the pride of the U.S Air Force's Strategic Air Command during the Cold War, the B-47 fleet meets a sobering end at this Davis-Monthan facility. **(R. F. Schirmer via AAHS Collection)**

The B-36s were physically large, but the B-47 was huge in numbers of aircraft. The first of more than 1,000 of the medium-range jet bombers began arriving in the desert in mid 1960. The Strategic Air Command's Project Fast Fly accelerated the B-47's retirement along with its KC-97 tankers. Fast Fly's retirement schedule called for 294 B-47s, 118 KC-97s, and 33 B-52s to be retired at a rate of four B-47s, two KC-97 tankers, and one B-52 per day. Although the KC-97s would fly with Air Guard units for a number of years to come, the propeller-driven tankers were being replaced by new, all-jet KC-135 Stratotankers. SAC's last B-47E arrived at Davis-Monthan on 11 February 1966, and it was followed on 29 December 1967 by the last RB-47H, serial number 53-4296—exactly 20 years after the type's first flight. When the B-47s underwent parts reclamation, all radar-recording cameras, each equipped with two film magazines, were saved for the Environmental Science Services Administration. B-47s were scrapped at a rate of 25 per month.

America's first double-sonic strategic bomber was retired due to escalating costs and lessons learned in the Vietnam War. The Convair B-58 Hustler was designed to penetrate Soviet airspace at twice the speed of sound, deliver its nuclear weapons, and depart the target area at high speed. Air combat over Vietnam showed that most modern aerial warfare would occur at "transonic"

Engine removal and other parts reclamation has begun in this early 1970s aerial view of the B-47 fleet. **(AMARG)**

Convair B-58A 59-2430 (right) sits at the back of the center row of Hustlers on the Davis-Monthan ramp. This was the 33rd Hustler to come down the Convair assembly line and was delivered on 10 February 1960. After nearly a decade of service, 59-2430 arrived at Davis-Monthan on 13 January 1970. **(AMARG)**

Built as a YB-58, 55-0670 made its first flight on 26 June 1958. This Hustler served as the cold-weather test aircraft at Eglin AFB from July to September 1958, and was subsequently converted to a TB-58 trainer configuration. The aircraft is seen fully cocooned on the Davis-Monthan ramp for a base open house in March 1971. (Harrison W. Rued)

Seen in April 1976, the B-58 Hustler fleet is awaiting its final disposition. By this time, the Vietnam War had ended and a number of 1950s-era Air Force aircraft were being added to the MASDC parking apron. One of the B-58s visible is 59-2444, known as Lucky Lady V. *Here, her luck was all but expended, and the Hustler was sold with the rest of the fleet to Southwestern Alloys on 27 May 1977, and subsequently scrapped. (Harrison W. Rued)*

Unidentified B-58 without pod sits in storage in March 1971. Note the yellow 3,000-pound weight used to maintain the aircraft's weight and balance. (Harrison W. Rued)

B-58A 59-2448 heads up one of the many rows of Hustlers, this one with a C/KC-97 (facing the camera in the background at left). (Harrison W. Rued)

speeds—ingress and egress of the target area at high speeds while slowing down to drop ordnance or engage in combat. Those lessons moved the B-58's phase-out ahead of schedule, and all aircraft were finally at MASDC by 16 January 1970, when 55-662 and 61-0278 arrived from the 305th Bomb Wing. Eighty-four aircraft were in storage, and only two aircraft escaped the smelter: B-58A 59-2442 (donated to the Pima Air & Space Museum)

and TB-58A 55-0668 (which eventually ended up at the Lone Star Flight Museum, Galveston, Texas). In 1976, the remaining Hustlers were sold as a single lot to Southwestern Alloys of Tucson, Arizona, for disposal.

A number of 1950s-era aircraft began arriving at MASDC in the 1971-1975 time-frame. Forty-four of the 50 Douglas C-133s built ended their days at MASDC, having begun to suffer fatigue problems as they

reached their expected flight life spans. The final Douglas C-124 Globemaster from the Air Force's inventory arrived from the 165th Tactical Airlift Group, Georgia Air Guard, in August 1974. Wing spar damage, the high cost of fuel, a shortage of R-4360 engine replacement parts, and the new jet-powered Lockheed C-141's ability to haul more cargo faster, all contributed to the grounding of the C-124.

When the early B-, C-, E-, and F-model B-52s had reached the end of their structural life spans, the fleet was flown to Davis-Monthan in late 1971. These aircraft wear the anti-flash nuclear paint scheme of silver upper and white lower surfaces. (Brian R. Baker)

Eerie afternoon shot among the more than 200 tall-tail B-52s awaiting their fate. (Nicholas A. Veronico)

From 1978 to 1982, the B-52D fleet was withdrawn to the desert. This sea of tall-tail B-52Ds, seen in July 1993, will only have to wait three more years before they are dumped into the scrapper's shredder and sold by the pound. (Nicholas A. Veronico)

Not even the Control Configured Vehicle testbed escaped the scrapper's torch. This highly instrumented NB-52E 56-0632 had canards attached below the cockpit floor and a rudder amidships just forward of the crew entrance hatch. This configuration was tested to improve the aircraft's handling qualities during high-speed, low-altitude flights. This configuration was never used on operational B-52s. (Nicholas A. Veronico)

The majority of the tall-tail B-52 fleet was sold to HVF West, which set up a shredding operation outside the fence near AMARC's southern border. Here B-52s were stacked two and three tall while they awaited their turn in the shredder. Once the aircraft were reduced to small pieces, about four inches by four inches, the scrap metal was loaded into open top rail cars and transported off site for smelting. (Nicholas A. Veronico)

B-52G 58-0165 was named Rolling Thunder *and saw extensive service during Operation Desert Storm flying from Morón Air Base, Spain. The aircraft is seen in 379th Bomb Wing's tribute markings as the wing wore the Triangle-K during World War II when it was equipped with B-17s. B-52G 58-0165 arrived at AMARC on 10 August 1992, and had been eliminated under the START treaty on 1 April 2001.* (Nicholas A. Veronico)

Boeing-Wichita B-52G 57-6475, Miami Clipper *(upper left corner), sits cut into five sections among a number of ex-93rd Bomb Wing, Castle AFB, California, Buffs.* Miami Clipper *was eliminated on 10 April 1996, and is seen the following month awaiting START treaty verification by Soviet satellite. During its career, 57-6475 had accumulated 12,652 hours flying time.* (Nicholas A. Veronico)

B-52G 58-0195, Eternal Guardian, *made its first flight on 2 September 1959. Thirty-four years later it was parked at AMARG after flying 13,680.9 hours while protecting the United States. The second aircraft in the row, 57-6520,* Ten Hi, *was parked in January 1994. It is interesting to note how certain internal parts from* Eternal Guardian *were salvaged in the most efficient manner—from the outside in—visible from the numerous cuts under and behind the cockpit.* (Nicholas A. Veronico)

B-52G 58-0224 *arrived at AMARG in February 1990 and occupies a parking spot among the B-52s to this day. The bomber last flew with the 43rd Strategic Wing, which was inactivated on 30 September 1990. The Stratofortress flew 13,079 hours before it was retired.* (Nicholas A. Veronico)

Aerial views of the B-52 fleet as the aircraft await their final fate, whether that is donating parts to keep other 50-plus-year-old Stratofortresses in the air or a date with the scrapper's torch. (Nicholas A. Veronico)

Originally, the B-52s were cut by dropping a 13,000-pound steel guillotine blade from the end of a crane boom from 80 feet in the air. The damage done by the guillotine blade is evident on 58-0243 (left), an ex-93rd Bomb Wing, Castle AFB, California, aircraft that arrived at AMARG on 11 June 1991, and was cut apart on 18 January 2001. The precision with which the former 416th Bomb Wing B-52G, 57-6516, *Ultimate Warrior* (below), was cut apart is evident in the clean edges on the wings and fuselage. To make the change in cutting methods, approval was sought from the Russians to avoid any suspicions when the aircraft were viewed on satellite photos. (Nicholas A. Veronico)

The death of the B-52 fleet was signaled on 21 July 1991, when the United States and the Soviet Union (now the Commonwealth of Independent States—Belarus, Kazakhstan, Russia, and the Ukraine) entered into the Strategic Arms Reduction Treaty (START). The treaty calls for each nation to reduce its nuclear-weapons-capable intercontinental and submarine-launched ballistic missiles and strategic bombers to 1,600. To meet this goal, a total of 365 B-52s were to be cut into five sections. Aircraft cut early in the program were reduced to five sections using a 13,000-pound blade dropped from a crane—one cut ahead of the wing root, one behind the trailing edge, and each wing severed. The broken B-52s were left in orderly piles for 90 days to allow satellite verification of the scrapping by the Commonwealth of Independent States. On 15 December 1994, the final two B-52Ds (56-0672 and 56-0614) fell to the chopping blade.

In the ensuing 15 years, it has become the B-52G's turn. The blade method does not make clean cuts and, in an effort to salvage as much as possible from the remaining B-52Gs, the Commonwealth of Independent States has agreed to allow AMARC to use a plasma saw to surgically cut the bombers into five pieces. On 24 July 2008, the first of 18 B-52Hs consigned to storage, 61-0023, left Minot AFB, North Dakota. B-52H 61-0023 was put into Type 1000 inviolate storage in case it is called back to active duty. The force drawdown of B-52Hs will see the active fleet reduced from 94 to 76 bombers, which will operate only from Minot AFB, North Dakota, and Barksdale AFB, Louisiana.

Parked side-by-side, both of these Starlifters were reduced to scrap on the same day. Ex-Travis AFB C-141B 65-0268 from the 60th Air Mobility Wing (AMW), foreground, arrived at AMARG on 21 April 1997. Ex-Altus AFB, Oklahoma, Starlifter 66-0205 from the 97th AMW arrived on 1 January 1997. Both aircraft, and many others of their type, were scrapped on 25 September 2003. (Nicholas A. Veronico)

It is an amazing sight to see so many Starlifters in one place. These stalwart aircraft flew the U.S. military to and from points all over the world during the Vietnam and Gulf Wars, and were seen nightly on TV returning American POWs, including future Senator and Presidential Candidate John McCain, from Southeast Asia. Perhaps the most noted of the POW repatriation aircraft was a C-141 named "Hanoi Taxi," now part of the permanent collection at the National Museum of the Air Force. (Nicholas A. Veronico)

Starlifter 61-2777 was the third C-141 built, and spent its service life testing various airborne systems and components for the Air Force. The large tail can was used to test different types of electronic countermeasures equipment being developed for the Rockwell B-1 and Northrop B-2. This C-141 was christened The Gambler for its triple-seven serial number. (Nicholas A. Veronico)

Aerial view of the Lockheed C-141 Starlifter parking area as the type began to arrive at AMARG. All of the aircraft wear camouflage paint schemes except for the 412th Test Wing's NC-141A 61-2777 seen near the top of the photo. All of the C-141s in this view have since been shredded. (Nicholas A. Veronico)

C-141B 63-8083 last served with the 57th Airlift Squadron, a component of the 443rd Airlift Wing based at Altus AFB, Oklahoma. This aircraft arrived in April 1996 and was sold for scrap in June 2003. Detail photo shows 63-8083's squadron insignia and white stenciled and spray-painted AMARG inventory number. (Nicholas A. Veronico)

Ex-Memphis-based 67-0029 last flew with the 164th Airlift Wing, Tennessee Air National Guard. The aircraft wears nose art of an eagle holding a sword with the words "Let's Roll" against the American flag in tribute to those who perished in the 11 September 2001, terrorist attacks. (Ron Strong)

C-141s were cut into large sections using the guillotine blade, with one cut into the fuselage between the wings and the tail, and then both wings were removed. The carcasses were removed from AMARG to the HVF West yard to be scrapped. (Dennis R. Jenkins)

At the contractor's yard, heavy equipment was used to reduce the aircraft into manageable sections. Seen here, a hydraulic shear is working its way through an unidentified Starlifter's wing box. A good, heavy-equipment operator can have this hulk smashed and loaded into a rail car in a matter of hours. (Dennis R. Jenkins)

The Lockheed C-141 Starlifter was the Air Force's first pure-jet cargo aircraft, and the stretched C-141B was capable of carrying 200 troops, 155 paratroopers, 103 litter patients with 14 aeromedical attendants, or 68,725 pounds of cargo. A total of 284 C-141s were built for the U.S. Air Force, and one additional aircraft, an L-300—the commercial version of the Starlifter—was acquired by NASA for use as an airborne telescope. In total, the C-141 fleet flew a combined 10.6 million hours, and each of the 251 aircraft sent to Davis-Monthan for storage averaged approximately 39,400 flight hours. The C-141s are cut into four sections using the guillotine blade; one cut on the rear fuselage separating the tail, and each of the wings removed.

One of the biggest fleets (and one that has been an on-going project for nearly 30 years) is the Boeing C/KC-135 Stratotanker program. Based on Boeing's revolutionary Dash-80 prototype jet transport, a total of 820 Stratotankers were built, 732 as refueling aircraft and 88 as cargo carriers and special-use aircraft. These aircraft flew airborne command post, electronic reconnaissance, and VIP transport missions.

Today the KC-135 is still the primary refueling aircraft for the U.S. Air Force, but that is about to change. Although the Air Force had accepted bids for a tanker replacement several years ago, acquisition of this new aircraft has been bogged down in a political quagmire. Many of the C/KC-135s flying today are nearing 50 years of service, and many will soon be added to the fleet currently in storage. In addition to the C/KC-135s, the Air Force acquired 104 commercial Boeing 707s and 720s between 1983 and 1990. These former airliners provided a valuable source of spare parts, engines, and tail assemblies for various C/KC-135 upgrade programs.

The aircraft that revolutionized commercial air travel, the Boeing 367-80 prototype jet transport, was a long-term resident at AMARG. Better known as the "Dash-80," it first flew in 1954 and served as the prototype for the larger Boeing 707 airliner and KC-135 Stratotanker. The aircraft arrived in 1972 and was visible to those on the AMARG tour for 18 years. In 1990 the Dash-80 was flown to Boeing's Seattle factory where it was refurbished. It was then flown to the Smithsonian Institution's National Air and Space Museum's Steven F. Udvar-Hazy Center located at Dulles Airport in Chantilly, Virginia. There, it became a centerpiece of the new museum annex when it opened in December 2003 in conjunction with celebrations for the 100th anniversary of flight. (John M. Campbell Collection)

To maintain and upgrade its KC-135 aerial-refueling tanker fleet, the U.S. Air Force acquired a large number of commercial Boeing 707s and 720s. The engines, tail assemblies, and other components were used to upgrade early KC-135s. On 11 April 1983, ex-Western Airlines Boeing 720-047B, N3162, arrived on the AMARG ramp. Note that the aircraft's airline markings have been painted over. After yielding all useable parts, this aircraft was scrapped in December 2001. (Nicholas A. Veronico Collection)

High-angle view of ex-African Express Airways Boeing 707-323B, N7158Z, manufacturer's serial number (msn) 20179, showing the removed vertical stabilizers sitting on the ground next to the aircraft. This 707 arrived at Davis-Monthan on 25 July 1990. (Nicholas A. Veronico)

N778TW (foreground), a Boeing 707-331B (msn 18409) was delivered to TWA on 21 February 1963. The aircraft was traded to Boeing for new equipment in March 1983, and was delivered to AMARG the following month. This aircraft has served as a source for spares for more than 25 years. (Nicholas A. Veronico Collection)

More than 190 Boeing 707 commercial airliners were acquired for the Air Force's KC-135 upgrade program. Typically parked 12 to a row, more than 65 different aircraft can be seen in these aerial photos. Once these aircraft were stripped of useable parts, their carcasses were sold to local scrappers and removed from AMARG. (Nicholas A. Veronico)

Still wearing its Pan Am livery, N885PA (msn 20024) was christened Clipper Northern Light *when it was delivered to the carrier on 1 January 1969. Pan Am leased the jetliner to Guyana Airways for an 11-month period beginning in June 1983 before the aircraft went to Davis-Monthan on 12 April 1984. The carcass was sold to scrapper HVF West on 12 June 1997.* (Nicholas A. Veronico)

Guyana Airways Boeing 707-321B N1181Z frames a stack of discarded vertical stabilizers and rudders. N1181Z arrived at AMARG on 20 February 1986. (Nicholas A. Veronico)

Parked in the aircraft battle damage repair (ABDR) area on the east side of AMARG is ex-TWA N28714 (msn 18408). This aircraft was delivered to TWA on 23 January 1963, as N776TW, and served uneventfully until 29 August 1969. On that date, members of the Popular Front for the Liberation of Palestine (PFLP) hijacked the aircraft believing that Yitzhak Rabin, Israeli Ambassador to the United States, was aboard. Rabin was not on the aircraft, however, and the hijackers had the jetliner flown to Damascus, Syria. Here the hijackers released all but two Israeli passengers (they would be held another four months until they were exchanged for Egyptian and Syrian POWs). The hijackers exploded a bomb in the cockpit of msn 18408 on 29 August 1969. The nose of British Overseas Airways Corporation's Boeing 707-465 G-ARWE (msn 18373), an aircraft that had suffered a fire destroying the fuselage, was salvaged and transported from London to Damascus. Here the new nose section was grafted to the TWA 707 (notice the pronounced seam between the nose and the fuselage, ahead of the spray-painted AMARG inventory number, CZ089). The aircraft was given the new registration of N28714 and continued to fly with TWA until arriving at Davis-Monthan on 16 December 1983. (Nicholas A. Veronico)

One of the biggest fleets of aircraft to be maintained at AMARG is the C/KC-135 fleet and its variants. KC-135A 56-3635, Yankee Clipper, *was delivered in March 1958 and flew until 25 August 1992, when it arrived at AMARG. It has subsequently served as a parts source for the C-135 fleet.* (Nicholas A. Veronico)

Former Utah Air National Guard KC-135E 59-1473 wears Special Olympics Utah *nose art in recognition of its participation in a Special Olympics charity event. On 11 August 2001, fifteen teams competed for the fastest time to pull this 145,000-pound KC-135 over a distance of 12 feet. A rope was attached to a tow bar hooked to the nose wheel, and the team from Home Depot won the contest. (Ron Strong)*

Former Beale AFB, California-based KC-135E, 57-1511, Lucky Leprechaun, *took up AMARG residence on 23 June 2004. (Ron Strong)*

KC-135E 58-0090 Eagle One *shortly after its arrival on the AMARG ramp on 27 March 2008. Note that the crew has signed the aircraft: "Thanks for the Memories" and "Sweet Dreams Ol' Gal. 50 Years Strong!!" (Ron Strong)*

KC-135E 58-0096 from the 940th Aerial Refueling Wing, Beale AFB, California, wears the nose art Honoring All Who Serve. *This aircraft arrived on 23 February 2004. (Ron Strong)*

EC-135P 55-3129 last served with the 6th Airborne Command and Control Squadron (ACCS), 1st Fighter Wing, at Langley AFB, Virginia. Prior to its service with the 6th ACCS, 55-3129 had been configured as an NKC-135E and flew parabolic flights to provide passengers with short periods of weightlessness. Those in the know say that 55-3129 has a bulkhead autographed by its passengers, including the Mercury 7 astronauts. This aircraft has been in storage since 31 January 1992. (Nicholas A. Veronico)

Awaiting its turn to be defueled is Utah Air National Guard KC-135E 59-1473, which arrived at AMARG on 6 March 2008. It is almost hard to believe that the KC-135 series has served the refueling needs of the U.S. Air Force and several foreign countries since the mid-1950s, having been augmented by only one other new aircraft since then, the larger McDonnell Douglas KC-10 Extender in 1981. (Ron Strong)

The Strategic Air Command maintained an airborne command post in the air— 24 hours a day, seven days a week, 365 days a year—from 3 February 1961 to 24 July 1990. The aerial command posts were nicknamed "Looking Glass" because the aircraft mirrored ground-based communications capabilities. The 55th Wing at Offutt AFB, Nebraska, was the last operator of an EC-135C, and 62-3585 was flown to storage on 2 June 1998. (Ron Strong)

OC-135B 61-2674 was part of the U.S. fleet of aircraft participating in the Open Skies Treaty. Signed 24 March 1992, this treaty enables nations to fly unarmed reconnaissance flights to gather military information about another Open Skies Treaty state. Flights are typically conducted with little notice in an effort to see as much as possible, and using aircraft enables countries without military satellite capabilities the opportunity to collect intelligence. OC-135B 61-2674 was last operated by the 55th Wing at Offutt AFB, Nebraska, and arrived at AMARG for storage on 21 August 1997. (Nicholas A. Veronico)

EC-135Y 55-3125 is a KC-135 that has been modified into an airborne command post for the commander-in-chief, U.S. Central Command. The tanker infrastructure was retained in the conversion and this aircraft is capable of off-loading fuel or being aerial refueled. It is powered by four Pratt & Whitney TF-33-PW-102 turbo-fan engines, and was the only aircraft converted to an EC-135Y configuration. The aircraft entered storage on 4 February 1999. (Nicholas A. Veronico)

America's largest aircraft, the Lockheed C-5 Galaxy, began arriving at AMARG at the end of 2003. The highest-time and least-reliable aircraft were retired first. Galaxy 66-8307 was the second of its type to arrive at AMARG, landing at the facility on 21 January 2004. (Ron Strong)

Aerial command post EC-135P 58-0022 arrived on 5 March 1992, from the 6th Airborne Command and Control Squadron, 1st Fighter Wing, at Langley AFB, Virginia. Note that the nose gear has been returned to the fleet. (Nicholas A. Veronico)

The Air Force's largest airlifter is the Lockheed-Martin C-5 Galaxy. This aircraft can carry nearly all of the U.S. Army's combat equipment from bases in the United States to any combat theater, anywhere in the world. With many of the Galaxies approaching 40 years of service, it was decided to invest in an upgrade of 47 C-5Bs and two C-5Cs (used to support the space program) with an avionics modernization program (AMP) that would remove all of the 1960s-vintage cockpit dials and replace them with a new, all-glass cockpit. Subsequently, the modernized C-5s would undergo a Reliability Enhancement and Re-engining Program (RERP). When all of the AMP and RERP upgrades are combined, it is anticipated that the C-5's reliability and dispatch rate will be greatly improved. The C-5 modernization program excluded an investment in the older C-5A airlifters. Of the 62 C-5As on strength, 13 were sent to AMARG for parts reclamation or storage. Many were immediately dismantled for parts to keep the others flying.

Seen on 14 April 2008, C-5A 67-0174 Legend of Sleepy Hollow *last served with the 105th Airlift Wing, New York Air National Guard. This aircraft was retired on 14 June 2005, and was the last of 13 C-5As sent to storage. The green cross spray-painted near the entry door indicates that all pyrotechnics (flares, etc.) have been removed from the aircraft, while the yellow "7" stenciled to the left of the AMARG inventory number (AACM0013) denotes that the aircraft's in-processing inspection has been completed.* (Ron Strong)

C-5A 67-0167 last flew with the 439th Airlift Wing, "The Patriot Wing" from Westover Air Reserve Base, Massachusetts, Air Force Reserve Command (AFRC). Westover set a record during Operation Iraqi Freedom when the base saw 1,103 C-5 departures between February and May 2003. The 439th sent C-5A 67-0167 to AMARG on 6 January 2005. (Ron Strong)

The C-5s in storage quickly gave up their horizontal stabilizers as parts were reclaimed for the flying fleet. (Ron Strong)

Some aircraft come apart quicker than others, depending on fleet demand for components. Here two C-5s show different levels of reclamation. While one has given up its outer wing panels and most of the front end including the cockpit, the second aircraft has had a wooden bulkhead with entry door fitted to the massive cargo bay opening. Both aircraft have surrendered their engines and engine pylons. (Ron Strong)

A C-5 nose cargo door has been prepared for immediate shipment should another aircraft need this component. (Ron Strong)

C-5 engine cowling sits in the Arizona sun against a backdrop of ex-Tyndall-AFB-based F-15 Eagles. (Ron Strong)

Rockwell B-1Bs from AMARG, including 86-0128, have donated large structural parts to help rebuild other B-1s. For example, in September 2005, an Ellsworth, South Dakota-based B-1B landed at Andersen AFB, Guam, and suffered a starboard landing-gear failure and resulting fire. The fire damaged the starboard wing, engine nacelles, and landing gear. These parts were removed from donor aircraft at AMARG, and sent by road to the Port of Los Angeles where they were shipped to the island outpost. Once the parts arrived at Guam, the rebuild commenced and the aircraft was returned to the B-1 fleet. One B-1B that was in storage, 86-0097, was returned to service at Dyess AFB, Texas, with the 7th Bomb Wing in September 2004, thus proving a flight into AMARG is not always a one-way affair.

From the smallest of helicopters to the hundreds of B-52s and the massive C-5s, AMARG manages all types of aircraft with the same professionalism and attention to detail.

Sweet Sixteen was the first Rockwell B-1B Lancer to arrive for storage. The aircraft, serial number 84-0056, landed at Davis-Monthan on 20 August 2002. A number of B-1Bs have undergone parts reclamation, including donating components to restore an aircraft that had an accident at Andersen AFB, Guam. (Nicholas A. Veronico)

Although capable of reaching speeds of Mach 1.2 at altitude, B-1B 85-0070 will never have that opportunity again, having donated many of its parts to keep other Lancers flying. Note both pilot seats sitting under the aircraft's left wing. This aircraft last served with the 77th Bomb Squadron, 28th Bomb Wing, Ellsworth AFB, South Dakota, and arrived at AMARG on 26 August 2002. (Ron Strong)

B-1B 86-0131, also from Ellsworth's 77th Bomb Squadron, 28th Bomb Wing, arrived at AMARG on 6 September 2002. Although the horizontal stabilizers have been removed, the actuating mechanism remains. Other salvaged parts await their return to the inventory. The large white tanks sitting next to the B-1Bs are internal fuel tanks that were located inside the aircraft's bomb bays. (Ron Strong)

B-1B 85-0062 sits on Celebrity Row representing the remaining 15 Lancers stored at AMARG (one had been returned to flying status). This aircraft was the second of the B-1B arrivals, landing at Davis-Monthan on 21 August 2002. (Ron Strong)

Rear three-quarter view of 86-0128 showing only one main landing gear truck. Note the AMARG-built aircraft cribbing that allows access to the underside of the aircraft. (Ron Strong)

Sealing the wing attach points, engine nacelles, and bomb bay preserves the myriad of parts located in these newly exposed areas. The main landing gear doors have been removed allowing greater access to the gear bays. Many of these parts went to repair B-1B 85-0066 that was involved in a landing accident at Andersen AFB, Guam, on 15 September 2005. (Ron Strong)

Preservation and cribbing details are evident in this starboard-side view of ex-Ellsworth Air Force Base B-1B 86-0128, which was the fifteenth of 17 Lancers sent to storage. The bomber arrived on 31 March 2003. The large curved-wing fairing is evidence that the B-1 is the Air Force's only variable-geometry four-engine strategic bomber. (Ron Strong)

Many consumable components have been removed and crated or palletized for shipment when needed. Here, brake assemblies and various gear doors have been stacked to await the call for duty. (Ron Strong)

B-1B 86-0128 wore Fury 1 nose art depicting a Lancer ascending against an eagle and American flag background. Note the last three digits of the aircraft's serial number on the nose gear leg and the South Dakota state outline on the nose gear door showcasing the crew's names. (Ron Strong)

B-1B 85-0092 last flew with the 128th Bomb Squadron, 116th Bomb Wing of the Georgia Air National Guard, based at Robins Air Force Base. The Lancer was named Apocalypse and wears appropriate nose art. (Nicholas A. Veronico)

B-1Bs face a line of B-52Gs with ex-7th Bomb Wing Lancer 84-0054 Rage *leading the row. This B-1B was delivered to the Air Force on 26 July 1986, and was flown to storage on 18 September 2002. (Nicholas A. Veronico)*

INVENTORY BY AIRCRAFT TYPE (2009)

Type	Count	Type	Count	Type	Count	Type	Count
A-1S	17	C-27A	4	FB-111	2	S-3	214
A-3B	11	C-123K	19	FB-111A	6	SH-2	40
A-4	153	C-130	162	GTD-21B	5	SH-60B	1
A-6	193	C-130H	5	H-1J	12	SP-2H	1
A-7	86	C-131B	2	H-3	12	SP-2H	2
A-7D	1	C-131F	1	H-3	66	T-1A	1
A-10	175	C-131F	9	H-46	61	T-2	125
AH-1J	1	C-137	1	H-53	88	T-33	8
AV-8A	1	C-137	50	HH-1	10	T-34	24
B-1B	16	C-140B	1	HU-25A	12	T-37B	375
B-52G	96	C-141	73	KC-135	187	T-38	160
B-52H	13	E-2C	26	LGM-25C	1	T-39	29
BGL-109A	8	EB/WB-57	9	MIG-15	1	T-39D	21
BGM-109G	2	EC-24A	1	MIG-17	2	T-39E	1
BGT-109A	1	F-3B	1	MIG-21	1	T-42	3
BQM-34F	1	F-4	40	MQM-13A	1	T-43	6
C-1A	17	F-4	400	NKC-135A	2	T-46A	1
C-2A	5	F-14	34	O-2A	26	TAV-8A	4
C-5A	13	F-15	160	OV-1D	5	TC-4C	7
C-9	6	F-16	417	P-3	2	TC-18E	2
C-9A	14	F-100F	1	P-3	137	TH-57A	4
C-12	19	F-101B	1	P-3B	1	UH-1	4
C-12C	2	F-111	8	PA-31T	1	UP-3B	1
C-21A	20	F-111	222	QF-106	2	US-2A	1
C-22	2	F/A-18	85	RF-8G	4	VH-34C	1
						Total	**4,288**

BONEYARD TOURS AND THE PIMA AIR & SPACE MUSEUM

Tours of AMARG are available for the general public through the Pima Air & Space Museum, 6000 E. Valencia Road, Tucson, Arizona. Tour buses depart the museum's entrance for AMARG Monday through Friday, excluding federal holidays. Cameras are allowed on the 60- to 90-minute narrated tour, and visitors must remain onboard the bus at all times. Reservations are recommended, and should be made at least seven days in advance by calling 520-618-4806. There is a small charge for the tour, which can be found on the museum's tour webpage (address below). Everyone over 16 years of age must present photo identification.

In addition to AMARG tours, the Pima Air & Space Museum has acquired one of the most diverse collections of military aircraft—many of which were formerly stored at AMARG. The museum was founded in 1966 by the Air Force Association's Tucson chapter, and in October 1969, 35 aircraft from the storage facility's Celebrity Row were transferred to the museum to form the basis of the collection. The museum and its collection of 75 aircraft formally opened to the public on 8 May 1976.

Today there are more than 275 aircraft in the collection that range from World War II-era bombers such as the B-17, B-24, and B-29 to the Century Series fighters—F-101,

An aerial image of the 309th Aerospace Maintenance and Regeneration Group's (AMARG) vast storage fields located on the Davis-Monthan Air Force Base in Tucson, Arizona. (U.S. Navy photo by Photographer's Mate 3rd Class Shannon R. Smith)

F-102, F-104, F-105, and F-106. The museum houses the VC-118 used by Presidents Kennedy and Johnson, as well as the supersonic B-58 and SR-71. The museum also has a snack bar and well-stocked gift shop. All public areas of the facility are handicapped accessible.

In May 1986, the Pima Air & Space Museum opened the Titan Missile Museum 25 miles south of Tucson (at 1580 W. Duval Mine Road, Green Valley, Arizona). Tours of the former Titan II Intercontinental Ballistic Missile (ICBM) in its underground silo show the complex as it was when operated by the U.S. Air Force's 390th Strategic Missile Wing. Visit the museum's website for tour times and prices. Additionally, Pima Air & Space Museum is the site of The Challenger Learning Center of the Southwest, which opened to the public in March 1999.

Additional information, events, and a listing of Pima Air & Space Museum aircraft can be obtained at www.pimaair.org.

BIBLIOGRAPHY AND SUGGESTED READING

Books

Andrade, John M. *U.S. Military Aircraft Designations and Serials Since 1909*. Midland Counties Publications. Earl Shilton, Leics., England. 1979.

Blanchard, Peter and Phillip Chinnery, Martyn Swann. *MASDC: Military Aircraft Storage & Disposition Center*. Aviation Press Ltd. London. 1983.

Bonny, Danny, Barry Fryer, and Martyn Swann. *AMARC—Aerospace Maintenance & Regeneration Center, Davis-Monthan AFB, Arizona 1982-1997 (MASDC III)*. Surrey, England. British Aviation Research Group. 2006.

Chinnery, Philip. *Desert Boneyard*. Airlife (England). 1987.

Chinnery, Philip D. *50 Years of the Desert Boneyard*. Motorbooks International. Osceola, Wisconsin. 1995.

Fryer, Barry and Martyn Swann. *AMARC—Aerospace Maintenance & Regeneration Center, Davis-Monthan AFB, Arizona 1982-1997 (MASDC II)*. London. Aviation Press Ltd. 1998.

Fugere, Jerry and Bob Shane. *Inside AMARC: The Aerospace Maintenance and Regeneration Center, Tucson, Arizona*. MBI Publishing Co. St. Paul, Minnesota. 2001.

Grantham, A. Kevin. *P-Screamers: The History of the Surviving Lockheed P-38 Lightnings*. Pictorial Histories Publishing Company. Missoula, Montana. 1994.

Johnson, Dave. *The Aerospace Maintenance And Regeneration Center*. LAAS International. West Drayton, Middx, England. 1995.

Knaack, Marcelle S. *Encyclopedia of U.S. Air Force Aircraft and Missile Systems: Post-World War II Bombers*: Washington, D.C. Office of Air Force History. 1988.

Larkins, William T. *Surplus WWII U.S. Aircraft*. Upland, California. BAC Publishers Inc. 2005.

Miller, Jay. *Convair B-58 Hustler: The World's First Supersonic Bomber*. Aerofax/ Midland Publishing Ltd. Earl Shilton, Leics., England. 1997.

Mitchell, S. and A. Eastwood. *Military Aircraft Serials of North America*. The Aviation Hobby Shop. West Drayton, Middx, England. 1991.

Mueller, Robert. *Air Force Bases, Volume 1*, Washington, D.C.: Office of Air Force History, 1989.

Pratt, Joseph A. and Castaneda, Christopher J. *Builders: Herman and George Brown*, College Station, Texas: Texas A&M University Press. 1999.

Thompson, Scott. *B-25 Mitchell in Civil Service*, Elk Grove, California: Aero Vintage Books, 1997.

Thompson, Scott. *Final Cut: The Post-War B-17 Flying Fortress*, Missoula, Montana: Pictorial Histories Publishing Company, 1990.

Veronico, Nicholas A. and Jim Dunn. *Giant Cargo Planes*. MBI Publishing Co. Osceola, Wisconsin. 1999.

_____. and Jim Dunn. *21st Century U.S. Air Power*. MBI Publishing Co. St. Paul, Minnesota. 2004.

_____. and A. Kevin Grantham, and Scott Thompson. *Military Aircraft Boneyards*. MBI Publishing Co. St. Paul, Minnesota. 2000.

Periodicals

Armstrong, William J. "Letter to the Editor (Clinton, OK)," *The Hook*, Spring 1983.

Baker, Brian. "Surplus Aircraft At Litchfield Park," *Journal of the American Aviation Historical Society*, AAHS, April-June 1958.

Birdsall, Steve. "Arizona Sundown," *Air Classics*, December 1969.

Bowers, Peter M. "The Saga of 5-Grand," *Wings*, June 1978.

Brinkley, Floyd. "White Elephants for Sale," *Air Force Magazine*, September 1946.

Cooper, Tom C. "Where B-52s Come Home to Roost," *Seattle Times Magazine*, September 19, 1971.

Dennison, Robert C. "Stratojet Swan Song," *Military Surplus Warplanes*, Fall 1997.

Kroger, William. "Junking of Old Planes Pressed Before 'Economy' Clamor Rises," *Aviation News*, November 26, 1945.

Larkins, William T. "Kingman, Arizona-1947: A Personal View," *Aerophile*, June 1979.

_____. "War Album," *The Aeroplane Spotter*, June 14, 1947.

_____. "Forgotten Warbird Graveyard," *Air Classics Quarterly Review*, Winter 1978.

_____. "War Assets: Part One," *Air Classics*, February 1992.

_____. "War Assets: Part Two," *Air Classics*, March 1992.

_____. "War Assets: Part Three," *Air Classics*, April 1992.

_____. "Return To Kingman," *Air Classics*, May 1997.

McLain, Jerry. "Warbirds' Swansong," *Arizona Highways*, May 1947.

Miller, J.J. and Guy Patterson. "Death Of An Air Force," *Flying*, November 1947.

Moll, Nigel. "Ghost Story," *Flying*, February 1989.

Montagnes, James. "Salvaging Our Surplus Warplanes—In Canada," *Flying*, September 1945.

O'Leary, Michael and Milo Peltzer. "Return To Kingman," *Air Classics*, May 1997.

Peck, Phillips J. "Salvaging Our Surplus Warplanes—In The U.S.," *Flying*, September 1945.

Peltzer, Milo and Michael O'Leary. "Ghosts of Litchfield Park," *Military Surplus Warplanes*, Fall 1997.

Schirmer, Col. Frank. "History of the 4105th AAF Base Unit, 1945-1948," *Journal of the American Aviation Historical Society*, AAHS, Spring 1986.

Sherman, Gene. "Warplanes Go to Arizona Desert to Die," *Los Angeles Times*, April 1, 1946.

Thompson, Scott. "Postwar Aircraft Disposal," *Journal of the American Aviation Historical Society*, AAHS, Winter 1992.

Documents

_____. *Disposal of Surplus Aircraft and Major Components Thereof*, Harvard University, May 22, 1945 (and reported to the Congressional Committee on Military Affairs, June 26, 1944).

_____. *Sale of Aircraft, Kingman, Arizona*, Subcommittee of the Committee on Expenditures in the Executive Department, U.S. Senate, June 4, 18-19, 1947.

_____. *War Wings for Peace*, Division of Information, War Assets Administration, 1946.

_____. *White Elephants With Wings*, Office of Surplus Property, undated.

_____. Statistical Information, Wunderlich Contracting Co., Sales as of Dec. 31, 1947.

Railing, Lawrence C. *Profile History: Military Aircraft Storage and Disposition Center and Predecessor Organizations, 1946-1974*: Davis-Monthan Air Force Base, Arizona. Air Force Logistics Command. 1975.

Trester, Dorothy W. *History of the AF Storage and Withdrawal Program (1945-1952)*, Historical Division, Office of Information Services, Air Materiel Command, Wright- Patterson AFB, Ohio, 1954 (available on USAF HRC microfilm reel #K2018).

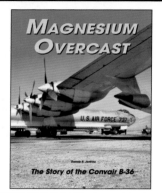

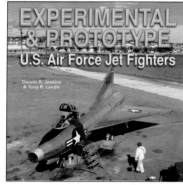

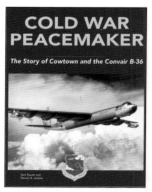